DYLAN

DYLAN

TEXT BY
JONATHAN COTT

DESIGNED BY
PAT STUPPI

A Rolling Stone Press Book

Doubleday & Company, Inc. • Garden City, New York 1984

Library of Congress Cataloging in Publication Data.

Cott, Jonathan.
Dylan.

"A Rolling Stone Press book."
1. Dylan, Bob, 1941– . 2. Singers—United States—Biography.
I. Title.
ML420.D98C67 1984   784.4'924 [B] 84-4049
ISBN 0-385-19161-8

Grateful acknowledgment is made for permission to reprint from: "The Crackin' Shakin' Breakin' Sounds" by Nat Hentoff, copyright © 1964 by the *New Yorker*; from *Playboy* magazine, March 1978, copyright © 1978 by *Playboy*; from *Positively Main Street: An Unorthodox View of Bob Dylan* by Toby Thompson, Coward-McCann, Inc. and Warner Books, Inc., copyright © by Toby Thompson; and from *Bob Dylan* by Anthony Scaduto, Grosset & Dunlap, Inc., copyright © 1971, 1974 by Anthony Scaduto.

Song lyrics: All compositions are used by permission. All rights reserved. Grateful acknowledgment is made to Dwarf Music for: "Absolutely Sweet Marie," ©1966 Dwarf Music, "All Along the Watchtower" ©1968 Dwarf Music, "Ballad of Frankie Lee and Judas Priest" ©1968 Dwarf Music, "I Want You" ©1966 Dwarf Music, "Obviously Five Believers" ©1966 Dwarf Music, "Just Like a Woman" ©1966 Dwarf Music, "Sign on the Cross" ©1971 Dwarf Music, "Stuck Inside of Mobile with the Memphis Blues Again" ©1966 Dwarf Music, "Tears of Rage" ©1968, 1970 Dwarf Music, "This Wheel's on Fire" ©1967, 1970 Dwarf Music, "Too Much of Nothing" ©1967, 1970 Dwarf Music; "Visions of Johanna" ©1966 Dwarf Music, "You Ain't Goin' Nowhere" ©1967, 1972 Dwarf Music; to Big Sky Music for: "If Not for You" ©1970 Big Sky Music, "I Threw It All Away" ©1969 Big Sky Music; to Ram's Horn Music for: "Wedding Song" ©1973, 1974 Ram's Horn Music, "Tangled Up in Blue" ©1974, 1975 Ram's Horn Music, "Never Say Goodbye" ©1973, 1974 Ram's Horn Music, "Dirge" ©1973, 1974 Ram's Horn Music, "Shelter from the Storm" ©1974, 1975 Ram's Horn Music, "Lily, Rosemary and the Jack of Hearts" ©1974, 1975 Ram's Horn Music, "You're Gonna Make Me Lonesome When You Go" ©1974, 1975 Ram's Horn Music, "Idiot Wind" ©1974, 1975 Ram's Horn Music, "Isis" ©1975, 1976 Ram's Horn Music, "Sara" ©1975, 1976 Ram's Horn Music; to Special Rider Music for: "Where Are You Tonight? (Journey through Dark Heat)" ©1978 Special Rider Music, "Señor" ©1978 Special Rider Music, "Every Grain of Sand" ©1981 Special Rider Music, "Saving Grace" ©1980 Special Rider Music, "When You Gonna Wake Up?" ©1979 Special Rider Music, "Slow Train" ©1979 Special Rider Music, "Property of Jesus" ©1981 Special Rider Music, "Do Right to Me Baby (Do Unto Others)" ©1979 Special Rider Music, "Don't Fall Apart on Me Tonight" ©1983 Special Rider Music, "Man of Peace" ©1983 Special Rider Music, "License to Kill" ©1983 Special Rider Music, "Neighborhood Bully" ©1983 Special Rider Music, "I and I" ©1983 Special Rider Music, "Precious Angel" ©1979 Special Rider Music, "When He Returns" ©1979 Special Rider Music; to Bob Dylan for: *Bringing It All Back Home* jacket notes ©1965 Bob Dylan, *Writings and Drawings* ©1973 Bob Dylan, *Joan Baez in Concert, Part 2* jacket notes ©1963, 1973 Bob Dylan, "My Life in a Stolen Moment" ©1962, 1973 Bob Dylan, "11 Outlined Epitaphs" ©1964 Bob Dylan, *Tarantula* ©1966, 1971 Bob Dylan; to M. Witmark & Sons for: "Don't Think Twice, It's Alright" ©1963 M. Witmark & Sons, "Like a Rolling Stone" ©1965 M. Witmark & Sons, "It's All Over Now, Baby Blue" ©1965 M. Witmark & Sons, "The Lonesome Death of Hattie Carroll" ©1964 M. Witmark & Sons, "One Too Many Mornings" ©1964, 1966 M. Witmark & Sons, "With God on Our Side" ©1963 M. Witmark & Sons, "Chimes of Freedom" ©1964 M. Witmark & Sons, "Blowin' in the Wind" ©1962 M. Witmark & Sons, "Who Killed Davey Moore?" ©1964, 1965 M. Witmark & Sons, "Only a Pawn in Their Game" ©1963, 1964 M. Witmark & Sons, "A Hard Rain's A-Gonna Fall" ©1963 Warner Bros., Inc., "Maggie's Farm" ©1965 M. Witmark & Sons, "It Ain't Me Babe" ©1964 M. Witmark & Sons, "All I Really Want to Do" ©1964 M. Witmark & Sons, "My Back Pages" ©1964 M. Witmark & Sons, "Restless Farewell" ©1964, 1966 M. Witmark & Sons, "Love Minus Zero/No Limit" ©1965 M. Witmark & Sons, "Mr. Tambourine Man" ©1964, 1965 M. Witmark & Sons, "Subterranean Homesick Blues" ©1965 M. Witmark & Sons, "It's Alright, Ma (I'm Only Bleeding)" ©1965 M. Witmark & Sons.

ACKNOWLEDGMENTS

Many people have contributed expertise, support, and time to help create this book.

Jonathan Cott would like to thank Jann and Jane Wenner, Jonathan Wells, Charles Parker, and Barbara Downey Landau; Jim Fitzgerald and Phil Pochoda of Doubleday; designer Pat Stuppi and photo editor Ilene Cherna; as well as Sarah Lazin, Elisa Petrini, Janis Bultman, Carrie Schneider, Holly George and Susan Murcko.

Robert McNamara, Mitchell Blank and Will Rigby offered advice and help, as did Rosemarie Sohmer, Peggy Allen, Dave Ridley and Kathleen Welch.

The editors of Rolling Stone extend their gratitude to all of these and to the many others whose talents and labors have made this project possible.

PREFACE

Talking about himself as a songwriter, Bob Dylan once said: "The words to the songs aren't written out just for the paper, they're written so you can read [them]. . . . If you take away whatever there is to the song—the beat, the melody—I could still recite it. . . . It ain't the melodies that're important, man, it's the words. I don't give a damn 'bout melodies."

The wonderful melodies of Bob Dylan's songs—drawing their inspiration from the singer's deep knowledge of and love for a wide range of music (including work and cowboy songs, country music, folk ballads, gospel, blues, R&B, rock & roll and reggae)—should never be underestimated. But in this essay on Dylan, I have intentionally focused on and emphasized the words of his songs, since I take Dylan to be primarily a poet who, in statement and in image, has kept alive the idea of the poet as *vates*—the visionary eye of the body politic—while at the same time keeping himself open to a conception of art that embraces and respects equally Charles Baudelaire and Charley Patton, Arthur Rimbaud and Smokey Robinson, Bertolt Brecht and Big Bill Broonzy. I have, therefore, drawn heavily on Dylan's own words as contained in three books—*Writings & Drawings* (1973), *The Songs of Bob Dylan* (1976), and *Tarantula* (his stream-of-consciousness novella, written in 1966)—as well as in several more recent songbooks and unpublished lyric sheets.

There have, of course, been innumerable books and articles published about Dylan. For invaluable information and ideas about his life and work I am indebted to a number of these books, in particular: *Bob Dylan,* by Anthony Scaduto, and *Positively Main Street,* by Toby Thompson (the two "unofficial" biographical works; Robert Shelton's long-awaited biography was unpublished at the time of my writing); *Bob Dylan: A Retrospective* (an excellent anthology, edited by Craig McGregor, of interviews with and essays about Dylan from the Sixties and early Seventies); *On the Road with Bob Dylan,* by Larry Sloman, and *Rolling Thunder Logbook,* by Sam Shepard (high-spirited accounts of Dylan's Rolling Thunder Revue tour); *Dylan—What Happened,* by Paul Williams (a short, sensitive rumination about Dylan's born-again Christian compositions); *Bob Dylan Approximately,* by Stephen Pickering (one of several books written or edited by this author, who views Dylan's work from the perspective of Jewish mysticism); and *Song & Dance Man: The Art of Bob Dylan,* by Michael Gray (a work that is especially insightful about Dylan's musical influences and the imagery of his songs). In 1978 Dylan gave unusually candid and lengthy interviews to Ron Rosenbaum for *Playboy* and to me for *Rolling Stone,* and I have drawn extensively on these as well.

I refer occasionally to unreleased Dylan recordings, but I have not dwelled on the riches of this important bootleg material. The basic books about these outtakes, demos, B sides, basement tapes, live performances, television and movie appearances, etc., are *Bob Dylan: His Unreleased Recordings,* by Paul Cable, and *Twenty Years of Recording,* by Michael Krogsgaard. People interested in this subject should also refer to *The Great White Answers,* by Dominique Roques, and to Greil Marcus's concise but brilliant commentary on the "unreleased Dylan" that originally appeared in the November 29, 1969, issue of *Rolling Stone.* Incidentally, CBS Records has had on-and-off-again plans to release a five-record set of some of this material, and may eventually get around to doing so. At this writing, however, some of Dylan's greatest songs—"She's Your Lover Now," "I'm Not There," "Caribbean Wind" and especially "Willie McTell"—are, unfortunately, still commercially unavailable. (Parenthetically, I should also mention Wanted Man, an English organization that publishes two newsletters, *The Wicked Messenger* and *The Telegraph*, which are often the first and the last word on every matter—from the sublime to the inane and from fact to hearsay—that has anything to do with Dylan.)

I am lucky enough to have seen Bob Dylan perform in Greenwich Village in the early Sixties; in Berkeley, California, in 1965, when he was accompanied by Joan Baez; in 1966 in England; on the Isle of Wight in 1969; and on every tour he has made since 1974.

In 1978, I interviewed Dylan twice—once in Los Angeles, just before the premiere of *Renaldo and Clara*, the next time in Portland, Maine, during a concert tour at the time *Street-Legal* was released. True to his reputation and to my image of him, Dylan was totally magnetic and mysterious, vulnerable and wary, sincere and caustic, witty and righteous, charming and sly. Indeed, he seemed to combine the characteristics of both the Joker and the Thief—the two characters he sang about in "All Along the Watchtower"—both of whose symbolic functions are to shake up one's preconceptions, received opinions, illusions and sense of security.

During one of my interview sessions with Dylan, I read him a text by the Hasidic rabbi Dov Baer, the Maggid of Mezeritch—a text that seemed to me to touch on Dylan's work. "From a thief," the Maggid had stated, "you should learn: (1) to work at night; (2) if one cannot gain what one wants in one night to try again the next night; (3) to love one's coworkers just as thieves love each other; (4) to be willing to risk one's life even for a little thing; (5) not to attach too much value to things even though one has risked one's life for them—just as a thief will resell a stolen article for a fraction of its real value; (6) to withstand all kinds of beatings and tortures but to remain what you are; and (7) to believe that your work is worthwhile and not be willing to change it."

Dylan responded: "That's the most mind-blazing chronicle of human behavior I think I've ever heard. . . . There's a man I would follow. That's a real hero. A real hero."

Throughout the years that I have listened to Dylan's records and seen him perform, he has seemed continually to change, yet somehow he has always remained who and what he is. When we had come to the end of the above interview, I asked him if he would autograph my copy of his *Writings & Drawings*. The page I chose for him to sign was the one on which the book's epigraph is printed: "If I can't please everybody / I might as well not please nobody at all / (there's but so many people / an' I just can't please them all)." And under that, Dylan wrote: "Jonathan, Do not take this statement at white face value—It might go like this: 'If I can't please everybody, I only might as well *might* please myself' . . . Just like that. Best Wishes and Good Luck, Bob Dylan."

—Jonathan Cott
New York City, Spring 1984

"There must be some way out of here," said the joker to the thief,
"There's too much confusion, I can't get no relief.
Businessmen, they drink my wine, plowmen dig my earth,
None of them along the line know what any of it is worth."

"No reason to get excited," the thief, he kindly spoke,
"There are many here among us who feel that life is but a joke.
But you and I, we've been through that, and this is not our fate,
So let us not talk falsely now, the hour is getting late."

—*"All Along the Watchtower"*

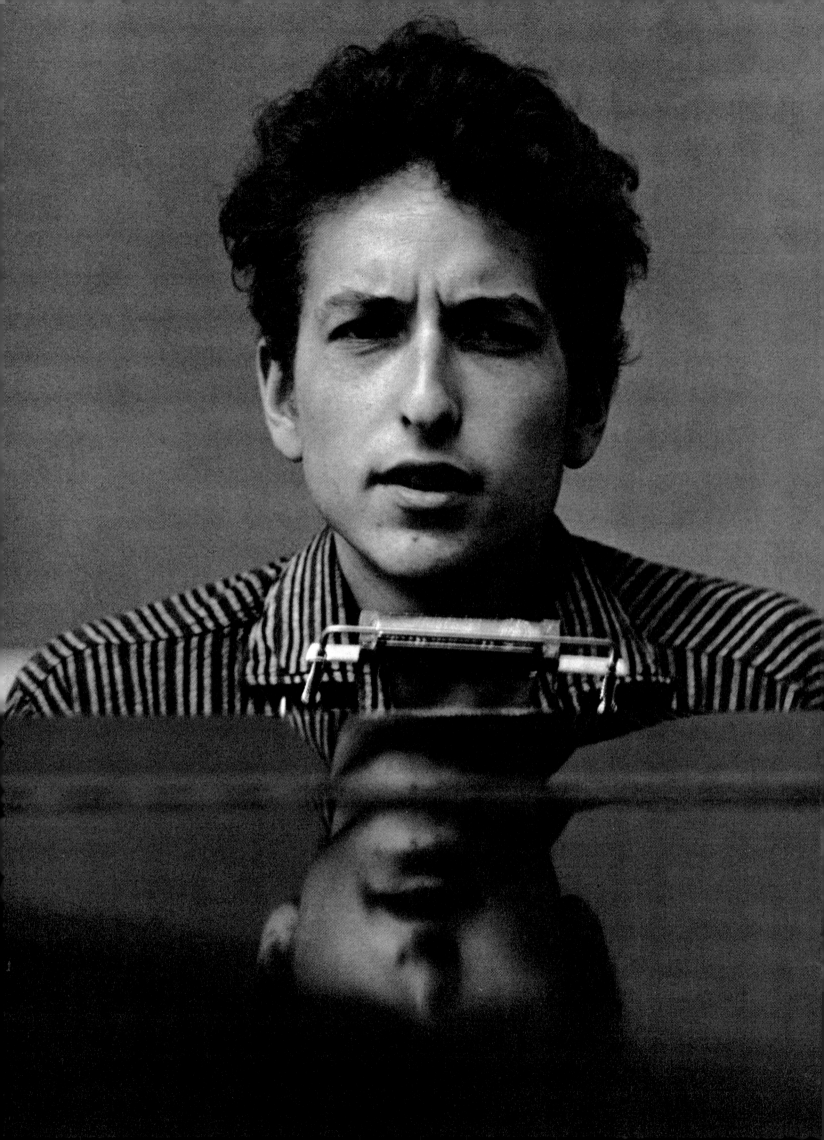

BOB DYLAN:
THE JOKER AND THE THIEF

e not busy being born / Is busy dying," Bob Dylan once sang in his song "It's Alright, Ma (I'm Only Bleeding)." And of his many memorable phrases, it is this one that might serve as his lifetime motto. For throughout his entire career, Bob Dylan has continually been busy being born and born again.

"Dylan used to tell us that he came out doing it, out of the womb, singing and playing and writing," recounted the late David Blue—("An' I sung my song like a demon child / With a kick an' a curse / From inside my mother's womb," Dylan wrote on his liner notes for *Joan Baez in Concert, Part 2*)—as if he were a legendary hero or an infant god.

His entrance into this world, however, was much more mundane. He was born with the name Robert Allen Zimmerman—the son of mortal parents, Abraham (Abe) and Beatrice (Beatty) Zimmerman—on May 24, 1941, in Duluth, Minnesota. At the age of six, he and his family, which now included his one-year-old brother, David, moved to nearby Hibbing (on the Mesabi Iron Range), where his father ran a hardware and appliance shop. By the time Robert was ten, he had informally taught himself the piano, learned the harmonica and, with some money he made "working on my daddy's truck"—as he once put it—bought a Silvertone guitar from Sears Roebuck, which, with the help of a book of chords, he began to play.

From his listening post up in the north country, he gradually absorbed the most vital elements of American popular music. He was first influenced by the records of Hank Williams ("my first idol," Dylan once called him). And later, he would tune in his radio to a station broadcasting out of Little Rock, Arkansas, where a disc jockey named Gatemouth Page played the music of Howlin' Wolf, B. B. King, Jimmy Reed, Chuck Berry and Little Richard. (Under Robert Zimmerman's high school yearbook picture is his goal: "To Join Little Richard.") Soon, Elvis Presley, Buddy Holly and other rock & roll masters were added to the pantheon.

In the eleventh grade he met a musical soulmate, Echo Star Helstrom ("Girl from the North Country"), who, to his amazement and delight, turned out to be a Gatemouth Page fanatic too. But he was equally appreciative of her mother's large collection of Forties and

1

Preceding page: Hibbing, Minnesota, Dylan's hometown. His father's hardware store was located here on the main street. This page: Dylan's persona when he arrived on the scene in Greenwich Village: part Huck Finn, part Charlie Chaplin, and part Woody Guthrie.

4

Fifties 78s of cowboy and country music songs; Bob would come over and listen to records by Hank Snow, Eddie Arnold, Pee Wee King and his Golden West Cowboys, and also to the Grand Ole Opry on the Helstroms' radio. He and some other high school friends then started getting together to play R&B and rock & roll at school assemblies, youth clubs and the occasional large auditorium, where their reception was often far from enthusiastic. No matter. Bob loved performing and paid little heed to the audience's occasional booing and laughter.

It is interesting to point out that even as a teenager, the singer not only was unfazed by uncomprehending criticism of his work but also seemed to encourage, and often thrived on, it. As he would say many years later, after having received some bad newspaper reviews of one of his tours: "It sort of makes me feel like the underdog. That fits me better anyway. I don't like being everybody's favorite. It makes you wonder if you're really saying anything at all." (On the other hand, he could sometimes feel betrayed if one of his friends made some slighting comment about his work. He once yelled at Phil Ochs—whom he kicked out of his limousine for saying something critical about one of his songs—"Get out, Ochs . . . you're not a folksinger, you're a journalist!")

By his senior year, he was spending some of his time with the biker crowd—he already had his own motorcycles (a Harley-Davidson was his first)—but his friends recall that he never really belonged to any one group, either the greasers or the establishment types. He was known as a "loner," and this seems to have been the way he was always thought of during his childhood and adolescence. In fact, this continued to be the case throughout his later life. He once said: "I won't join a group. Groups are easy to be in. I've always learned the hard way. . . . When you fail in a group you can blame each other. When you fail alone, you yourself fail."

Dinkytown, the bohemian section of Minneapolis where Bob had gone to attend the University of Minnesota. "Bob Dylan" first appeared in a coffeehouse here named The Ten O'Clock Scholar, playing guitar and singing for small change. Next page, left: Woody Guthrie, Dylan's "last idol."

6

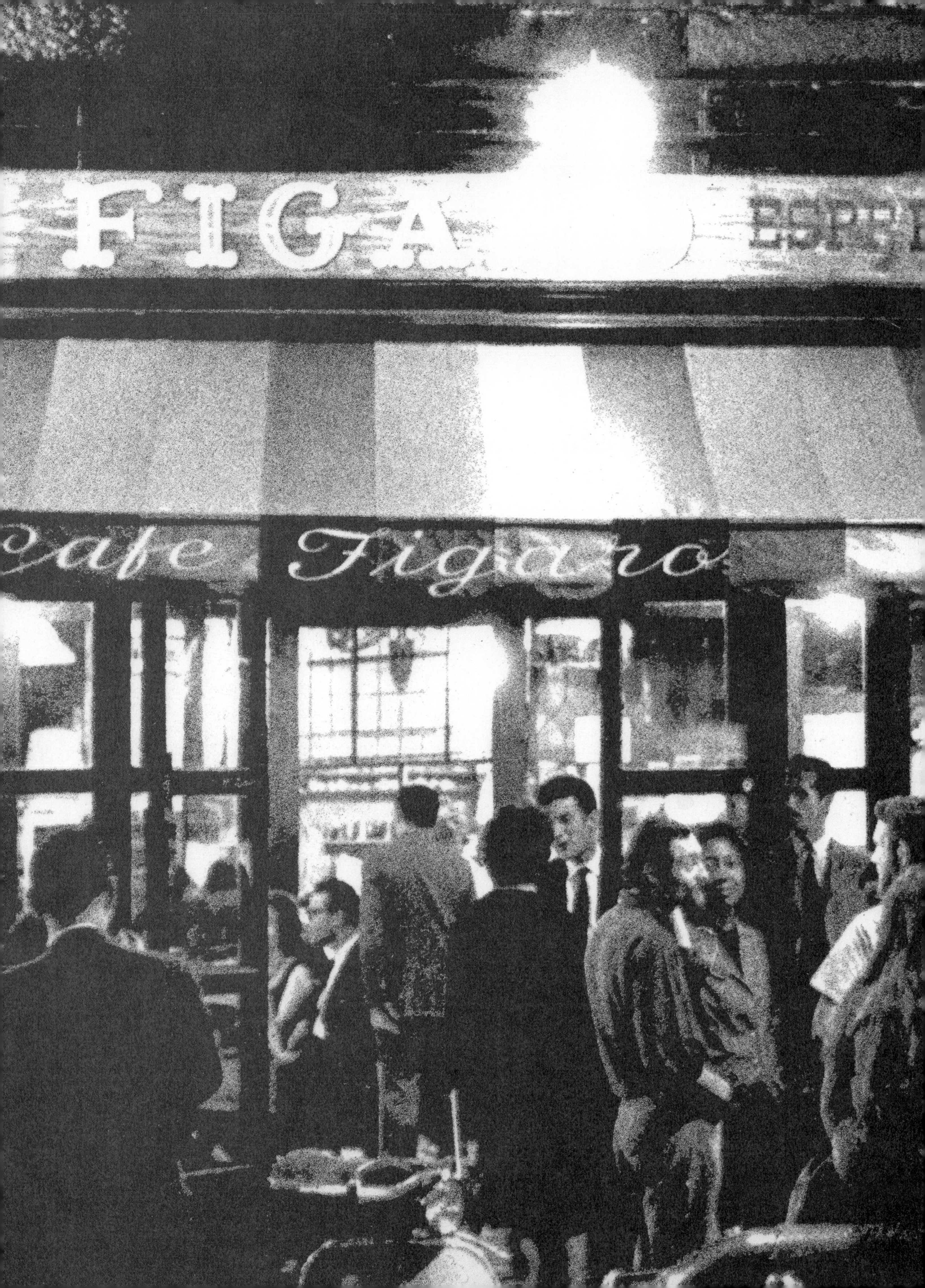
FIGA
Cafe Figaro

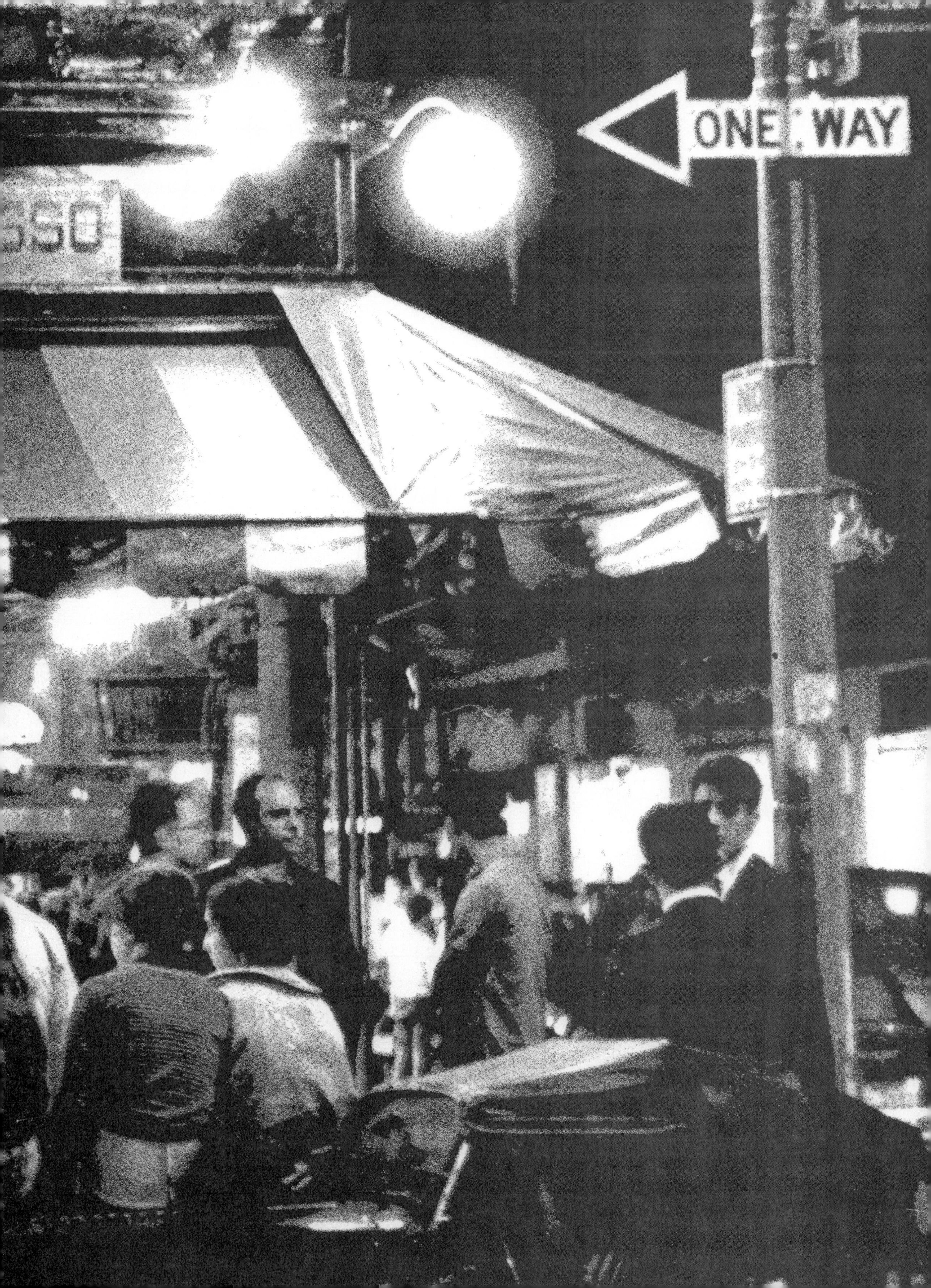
ONE WAY
550

"He was a real quiet boy," the Zimmermans' baby sitter, Don Mckenzie, recalled to journalist Toby Thompson in 1968—twenty years after he had taken care of a seven-year-old Bobby Zimmerman. "His brother David hadn't broken in his first pair of diapers, and already you could tell that he was going to be the extrovert of the two. Bobby stayed quiet, friendly, but, well, kind of *slinky* the whole time he was growing up. Used to write poems . . . don't know if he still does or not. But whenever Mother's Day or Father's Day or somebody's birthday rolled around, Bob would have a poem ready."

Toby Thompson also tracked down Robert Zimmerman's high school English teacher, B.J. Rolfzen, who confirmed that Robert was a "quiet boy, aloof." Thompson related that he "used to sit in the front row of B.J.'s class, to the left of the desk. Never said a word, just listened. Got good grades, B-plusses. . . . Took life seriously. Spent a lot of time by himself, must have been thinking and writing."

One of the biggest shocks of B.J.'s life, as Thompson recounts it, was the first time Robert and his band performed at a school concert. "Eleventh grade, the Jacket Jambourie Talent Festival. Curtain went up, Robert gave the signal, and *absolutely* the loudest music anybody had ever heard . . . and Robert! *Standing up* at the piano, screaming this . . . music into three microphones, this quietest of boys from the front row of B.J.'s English class. . . . Positively Dionysian! That silent boy. And the way he acted the next day! Sat down in his usual seat there in the front row of B.J.'s English class, didn't say anything, but . . . smirked the entire period. As if to say, 'That's right, B.J. You saw it. And you can be a witness.' "

There seems to be only one reliable witness to the birth of Robert Zimmerman's new incarnation as "Bob Dylan," and that is Echo Helstrom. According to her, during their junior year in high school, "Bob came over to my house after school one day and told me he'd finally decided on his stage name. Yes, it was Dylan . . . after the poet, I think."

The Cafe Figaro (preceding page) and Cafe Wha? (above) were important stops on the folk circuit in the early Sixties. Right: Dave Sears plays banjo in Washington Square Park, which was, in Dylan's words, "a place where people you knew or met congregated every Sunday and it was like a world of music."

Years later, when asked by Anthony Scaduto—Bob Dylan's unofficial biographer—to confirm this, Dylan replied that as far as he remembered, it had actually been about two years later that he had asked a man named David Lee, who owned a coffeehouse called The Ten O'Clock Scholar in the bohemian Dinkytown section of Minneapolis, if he could play guitar there sometime. (After graduating high school, Dylan had attended classes at the University of Minnesota for one semester in 1959.) Lee had finally agreed, offering him no payment, but asking his name. And Robert Zimmerman had replied, "Bob Dylan." "I needed a name in a hurry," Dylan explained to Scaduto, "and I picked that one. It just came to me as I was standing there in The Scholar. He asked me how he should bill me, and the name just came to me. Wasn't Dylan Thomas at all, it just came to me. I knew about Dylan Thomas, of course, but I didn't deliberately pick his name."

"It's a common thing to change your name," Dylan told *Playboy* in 1978. "It isn't that incredible. Many people do it. People change their town, change their country. New appearance, new mannerisms." But there seem to have been existential motives as well as a nonchalant entertainers-do-this-all-the-time attitude involved in this change. As he told me, also in 1978, "I didn't create Bob Dylan. Bob Dylan has always been here . . . always was. When I was a child, there was Bob Dylan. And before I was born, there was Bob Dylan. . . . Sometimes your parents don't even know who you are. No one knows but you. Lord, if your own parents don't know who you are, who else in the world is there who would know except you?"

Whatever the explanation(s),* it is clear that "Bob Dylan" was in the process of being born

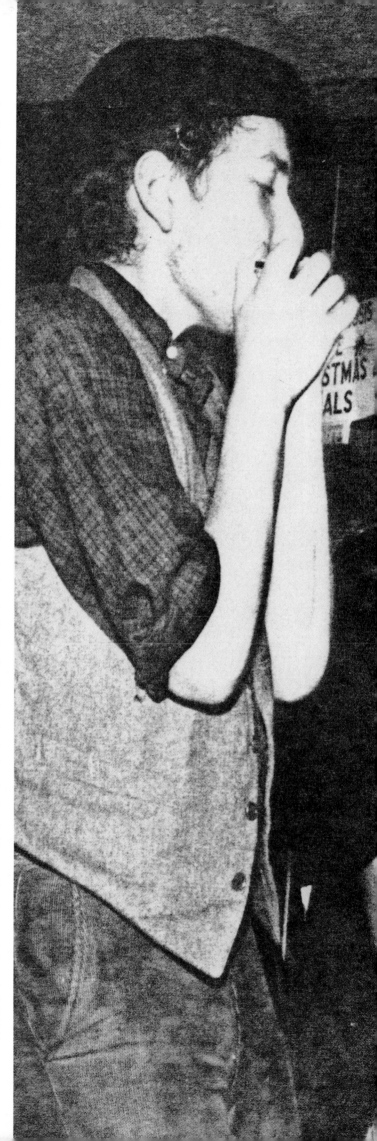

Dylan, Karen Dalton and Fred Neil at the Cafe Wha?, 1961. Dylan was playing in Village coffeehouses to get some exposure and Fred Neil was one of the first to pay Dylan to share club dates with him.

*As the Mexican poet Octavio Paz writes: "The poetic experience, like the religious one, is a mortal leap: a change of nature that is also a return to our original nature. Hidden by the profane or prosaic life, our being suddenly remembers its lost identity; and then that 'other' that we are appears, emerges."

sometime between 1957 and 1959. It was also during this period, incidentally, that he traded in his electric guitar and amplifier for a flattop Gibson acoustic guitar, an act inspired by his having heard an album of Odetta's. He learned all the songs on that record, which included "Mule Skinner," "Jack of Diamonds," "Water Boy," and "'Buked and Scorned." And from Odetta he moved on to the Carter Family, Jesse Fuller, Leadbelly and, finally, to Woody Guthrie. People have accused Dylan of latching on to the folk-music revival as a way of breaking into the music scene in Minneapolis and New York City. But as he once told a friend: "I had just made up my mind very early that if there was anything you wanted, you really had to make an attempt to sacrifice everything, a lot of things. . . . I was about seventeen, eighteen, and I knew there was nothing I ever wanted, materially, and I just made it from there, from that feeling. But then I realized I couldn't make it with a group . . . I had to do it alone. So I decided to do it alone through the folk thing." And as he later added: "My life is the street where I walk, that's my life. Music, guitar, that's my tool."

To his frat-house roommates (he lived for a short time at Sigma Alpha Mu) and college classmates he was Bob Zimmerman, but in Dinkytown he was now passing himself off as Bob Dylan. One of his friends of that time, Ellen Baker, recalled: "I used to ask him, 'How's the man of the soil today?' And that's what he was. Full of the Jesse Fuller thing, being down to earth, being a man of the soil. When all the time he was the son of a Jewish furniture dealer from up on The Range. The funny thing is, there's a certain mystique about being from The Range, an honorable thing, tough, mine-working, hardy people up there. People from The Range were proud of it. But Bob would rather have been from some place in Arkansas. He wanted to be part of another kind of romantic and glorious tradition . . . some sort of folk Dust Bowl tradition."

Above: Dylan's first paid New York club gig is announced by a sign in the window of Gerde's Folk City, Greenwich Village. Originally a jazz club, Gerde's had become the preeminent folk club by the time Dylan arrived there in 1961. Right: Dylan in an appearance at Gerde's popular Monday night hootenannies. Next page: With Suze Rotolo, who Dylan called "the true fortune-teller of my soul" and who appears on the cover of The Freewheelin' Bob Dylan.

16

And beginning at that time, under the enormous influence of Woody Guthrie, his music and his "hard travelin' " ways, Bob Dylan began to *create* a self for himself, much as a novelist creates a character. The American writer Laura Riding in *Progress of Stories* best describes this process in her description of a Miss Banquett, who was beautiful only because others thought her so. One day she decided to be beautiful for her *own* sake. So, by herself, and on her own, she began to write the book of her life. And, as Laura Riding states it: "Here all was different. For, although she read out of a book, it was a book of her own making. She knew that her name meant herself. Or, we might say, in the one book her beauty was factual—that is, of others' making, and therefore false; while in the other it was fictional—that is, of her own making, and therefore true. But it was indeed a very odd life that she now led. And yet not odd."

"Odd" is a mild way of describing the ever-shifting account Dylan gave of his origins and personal history to his friends and colleagues in New York City when he arrived there in 1961. According to him, he had run away from home on various occasions, the first time being at the age of ten when, he claimed, he wound up meeting Woody Guthrie in Califor-

nia. He said he had worked as a circus hand, a carnival boy, traveled as a road hustler and rode freight trains, then moved around as a street singer through the towns and cities of America where, he further asserted, he had met and learned songs personally from Mance Lipscomb, Arvella Gray, Jesse Fuller and Big Joe Williams. And, according to him, he had Indian blood and had taken the name "Dylan" from his mother's brother, who was a Las Vegas gambler. At other times, he gave out the story that he was an Okie.

Like other mythological heroes, Bob Dylan also claimed to have been an orphan—after all, as "Bob Dylan" he *had* no parents. A woman friend of his in New York recalled: "I once said, 'Bobby, what about your parents? Where are they?' And he said, 'I had so many different foster parents, I don't remember.' I said, 'Oh, you did? What was the name of your last foster mother?' He said, 'I don't rightly remember.' " In a remarkable way, he combined the characteristics of Huck Finn and those of another orphan, James Dean, with whom many young people at the time were identifying themselves, adulating what film director François Truffaut saw as that actor's "continual fantasy life; moral purity without relation to everyday morality, but all the more rigorous; eternal adolescent love of tests and trials; intoxication, pride and regret at feeling oneself 'outside' of society; refusal and desire to become integrated; and, finally, acceptance—or refusal—of the world as it is." As Dylan himself once said appreciatively of James Dean, "He let his heart do the talking."

And in his all-fusing character and his mythical re-creation of his past—he had made up for himself his own Great Depression and Dust Bowl to wander through—Bob Dylan was making a fiction true to his heart and true to the reality of his imagination. Those who believe that fiction is always false took Dylan to be nothing but a fool, but he had indeed be-

Above, left: In the studio with blues great Victoria Spivey in 1961: Dylan made one of his first studio recordings with her and Big Joe Williams. Right: Dylan submitted a number of songs—many still unrecorded—to Broadside, *a forum for songwriters.*

come the "mystery tramp," the "juggler," the "clown," the "Napoleon in rags"—all embodiments of the Fool—he would sing about in his song "Like a Rolling Stone." It is this character who, through laughter, cunning and the appearance of madness, enabled him to see through the illusions of his own personality and the world's.

In one of Kierkegaard's parables, a man in seventh heaven meets the Greek god Hermes (known to the Romans as Mercury), who offers the man the gift of youth or beauty or power or a long life. The man says to Hermes, "I choose this one thing, that I may always have the laugh on my side." And Hermes, himself laughing, grants the man his wish. In a way, we might suggest that Bob Dylan, like all wise and laughing fools, has always been under the protection of this trickiest of the gods—the "crafty," "deceiving" and "ingenious" Hermes (these were the epithets applied to this god).

Significantly, Hermes was, among other things, the patron of thieves. "Why must I always be the thief?" Dylan sings plaintively in "Tears of Rage." But for Dylan, the "thief"—a character who appears in a number of his songs—is usually depicted not as a desperate and lonely person but rather as an often deceptive but courageous and righteous loner-outlaw ("To live outside the law you must be honest," he sang in "Absolutely Sweet Marie"). And as he would later sing about Jesus: "Like a thief in the night / He'll replace wrong with right" ("When He Returns"). In this light, it is interesting to recall that on the day he was born, the first thing Hermes did was steal his brother Apollo's cattle.

But Hermes was also the inventor of the lyre and the shepherd's pipe, the epitome of the power of the spoken word, a guileless perjuror, the god of borderlines (external and internal) and the Lord of the Roads (both geographical and psychological). As the

In 1961, Dylan became the first of the younger male folk artists to be signed by a record company when John Hammond (above and right) of CBS Records gave him a contract shortly after meeting him and seeing him perform. Hammond is something of a legend in his own right, having signed such artists as Count Basie, Billie Holiday and, later, Bruce Springsteen to CBS. At the time, however, some CBS executives were skeptical of Dylan's potential and referred to him as "Hammond's folly."

*Dylan's early sessions at CBS.
Next page: Journalist Al
Aronowitz, producer Tom
Wilson and, far right, Albert
Grossman. Grossman became
Dylan's manager after he
recorded his first LP.*

scholar Walter F. Otto has written about him in *The Greek Gods*: "It is in [Hermes's] nature not to belong to any locality and not to possess any permanent abode; always he is on the road between here and yonder, and suddenly he joins some solitary wayfarer."

And when the curly-haired Bob Dylan first appeared in New York City with his guitar and mouth harp—wearing his Huck Finn cap (his version of the fool's cap) and his motley clothes (an undersized jacket and oversized boots), and sounding like Woody Guthrie (explaining that he had picked up his accent from an old black street singer he'd met in New Mexico)—he gave the appearance of a child hobo, a little boy lost, raw, innocent and vulnerable. As the singer Victoria Spivey described him at the time: "He was so meek and so humble, like a pet, just like a little baby boy. A poor little baby, a tiny little thing. He was the kind of boy you wanted to pull the sleeve on his sweater down so it looked right, or straighten his tie, except he didn't wear a tie. But he was a no-talking man. He didn't talk about nothing, or, when he did talk, he talked in riddles. Jive talk, always jiving. That was Bobby Dylan."

In fact, according to Bob's mother (whom Toby Thompson interviewed in 1969), while playing the little boy lost, Bob had actually gone to New York City "with our blessing. And as for losing track, or not keeping in touch . . . he was in New York two days when he called back to ask if David had been shoveling the walk. He's like that, your Bob Dylan, he has always cared about his family more than himself; he would do anything."

Ordinarily we would call such a person "two faced," at the very least. It is interesting, however, to recall that the first known troubadour poet, the eleventh-century Guillaume IX, was known as a *trovatore bifronte*—a poet with two faces. But singing poets typically have even more than two faces, *not* because they are hypocrites, but simply because, as the medieval

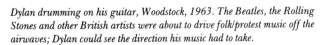

Dylan drumming on his guitar, Woodstock, 1963. The Beatles, the Rolling Stones and other British artists were about to drive folk/protest music off the airwaves; Dylan could see the direction his music had to take.

scholar Frederick Goldin suggests, they are performers.

Like Guillaume IX, Bob Dylan—a modern-day performing troubadour—also revealed many faces and voices. The singer Kris Kristofferson once said of him: "He's a dozen different people." And another of Dylan's friends commented that "there's so many sides to Dylan, he's round!" Anthony Scaduto, among others, has asserted that Bob Zimmerman "built a new identity every step of the way in order to escape identity." Now, it is certainly true that in his songs and interviews Dylan often talked about his need to "hide." As Frankie Lee tells Judas Priest: "Would you please not stare at me like that . . . / It's just my foolish pride, / But sometimes a man must be alone / And this is no place to hide" ("The Ballad of Frankie Lee and Judas Priest"). Or, as the singer once told an interviewer: "The sound of my own voice . . . I can't get used to it, never have gotten used to it. Makes you wanna *hide*." But it might be just as interesting to surmise that the creation of Bob Zimmerman's new self actually allowed him to distance himself enough from his home environment—"past the city limits," as he once wrote—in order to explore and develop his many selves and affinities, both musical and otherwise. (He once wrote: "an' just let me be me / human me / ruthless me / wild me / gentle me / all kinds of me.") As such, the creation of "Bob Dylan" might be seen as an experiment in self-creation and, more important, in self-discovery and self-revelation—a conjuring-up and probing and testing out of his personality. (At a concert in New York City on October 31, 1964, Dylan at one point told his audience, "It's Halloween and, uh, I've got my Bob Dylan mask on." Wearing a mask, of couse, allows one to hide, but it also makes it unnecessary to hide, since in the security of the disguise, one can let one's true self show.)

In his book *Song & Dance Man: The Art of Bob Dylan*, the English writer Michael Gray states: "What Dylan does not do . . . is consciously to offer a sustained, cohesive philosophy of life, intellectually considered and checked for contradictions. What he does offer is the artistic re-creation of the individual's struggle in our times." While Dylan's entire career certainly reflects this struggle, it also, I think (except during the period when he became a born-again Christian), *does* offer a generally consistent and often adamantly held "philosophy of life." From his songs, prose and poetic writings of the early Sixties right through to the extensive interviews he gave to *Rolling Stone* and *Playboy* in 1978, Bob Dylan always insisted that one had to make and take one's own path and to write the book of one's own life for oneself. (As he sang in "One Too Many Mornings," "Everything I'm a-sayin' / You can say it just as good.") And, as he told *Playboy* about "certain truths" that he had acquired on the road: "One is that if you try to be anyone but yourself, you will fail; if you are not true to your own heart, you will fail." He came to this realization early on while growing up in what was by all accounts the confining, conforming and closed-minded environment of a small Midwestern town during the scarcely rebellious Fifties:

Hibbing's got schools, churches, grocery stores an' a
*   jail*
It's got high school football games an' a movie house
Hibbing's got souped up cars runnin' full blast on a
*   Friday night*
Hibbing's got corner bars with polka bands
You can stand at one end of Hibbing on the main
*   drag an' see clear past the city limits on the*
*   other end*
Hibbing's a good ol' town
                    —"My Life in a Stolen Moment"

But however stultifying Hibbing appeared from the outside, the surrounding countryside also offered a landscape of visions for those who could see them. As Dylan would recount in *Playboy* magazine in 1978: "In the winter, everything was still, nothing moved. Eight months of that. You can put it together. You can have some amazing hallucinogenic experiences doing nothing but looking out

Preceding pages: Dylan once said: "My life is the street where I walk. Music, guitar, that's my tool." Here, he's on the street with Suze Rotolo, Dave Van Ronk and Van Ronk's wife Terri, New York, 1963.

Left: Dylan with Victor Maimudes, his official road manager and bodyguard, 1963. Maimudes was part of the entourage that protected him from clutching fans.

It was Dylan's harmonica playing that got him his first studio work, on a Harry Belafonte session. He ended up on only one cut because he couldn't stand to play things over and over.

Oh my name it is nothin'
My age it means less
The country I come from
Is called the Midwest
I's taught and brought up here
The laws to abide
And that land that I live in
Has God on its side.

And shortly thereafter he wrote in his *11 Outlined Epitaphs* (which first appeared on the cover of *The Times They Are A-Changin'*):

an' every action can be questioned
leavin' no command
untouched an' took for granted
obeyed an' bowed down to
forgettin' your own natural instincts. . . .

an' I stand up an' yawn
hot with jumpin' pulse
never tired
never sad
never guilty
for I am runnin' in a fair race
with no racetrack but the night
an' no competition but the dawn. . . .

an' mine shall be a strong loneliness
dissolvin' deep
t' the depths of my freedom
an' that, then, shall
remain my song

your window. There is also the summer, when it gets hot and sticky and the air is very metallic. There is a lot of Indian spirit. The earth . . . is unusual, filled with ore. So there is a magnetic attraction there. Maybe thousands and thousands of years ago, some planet bumped into the land there. There is a great spiritual quality throughout the Midwest. Very subtle, very strong, and that is where I grew up." His confrontation with conformity, combined with an intense imaginative life, a love for different kinds of authentic American music and musicians, a deeply felt sympathy for laid-off and often dispossessed miners, and a feeling of being somewhat of an outsider as a Jew, all contributed to an inner-directed personality that would make Dylan observe and comment about things, people and events in a way that was free of dogma, cant, prejudice and unthinking patriotic values. As he announced ironically in his song "With God on Our Side":

Here, then, was an artist who was going to take seriously Walt Whitman's great and inspiring advice from the Preface to his *Leaves of Grass*: "This is what you shall do: . . . Stand up for the stupid and crazy . . . hate tyrants . . . take off your hat to nothing known or unknown or to any man or number of men, go freely with powerful uneducated persons and with the young and with the mothers of families . . . reexamine all you have been told at school or church or in any book, dismiss whatever insults your own soul, and your very flesh shall be a great poem and have the richest fluency not only in its words but in the silent lines of its lips and face and between the lashes of your eyes and in every motion and joint of your body."

Hootenannies were a popular form of entertainment, where struggling musicians and poets could get up and try out their material. Right: With Mark Spoelstra at the Indian Neck Folk Festival, May 6, 1961.

Dylan and friend in a peaceful moment. Next page: Some of the approximately 46,000 people, many of whom had come expressly to see Dylan, at the Newport Folk Festival, 1963. It was the largest and youngest crowd ever to attend the festival.

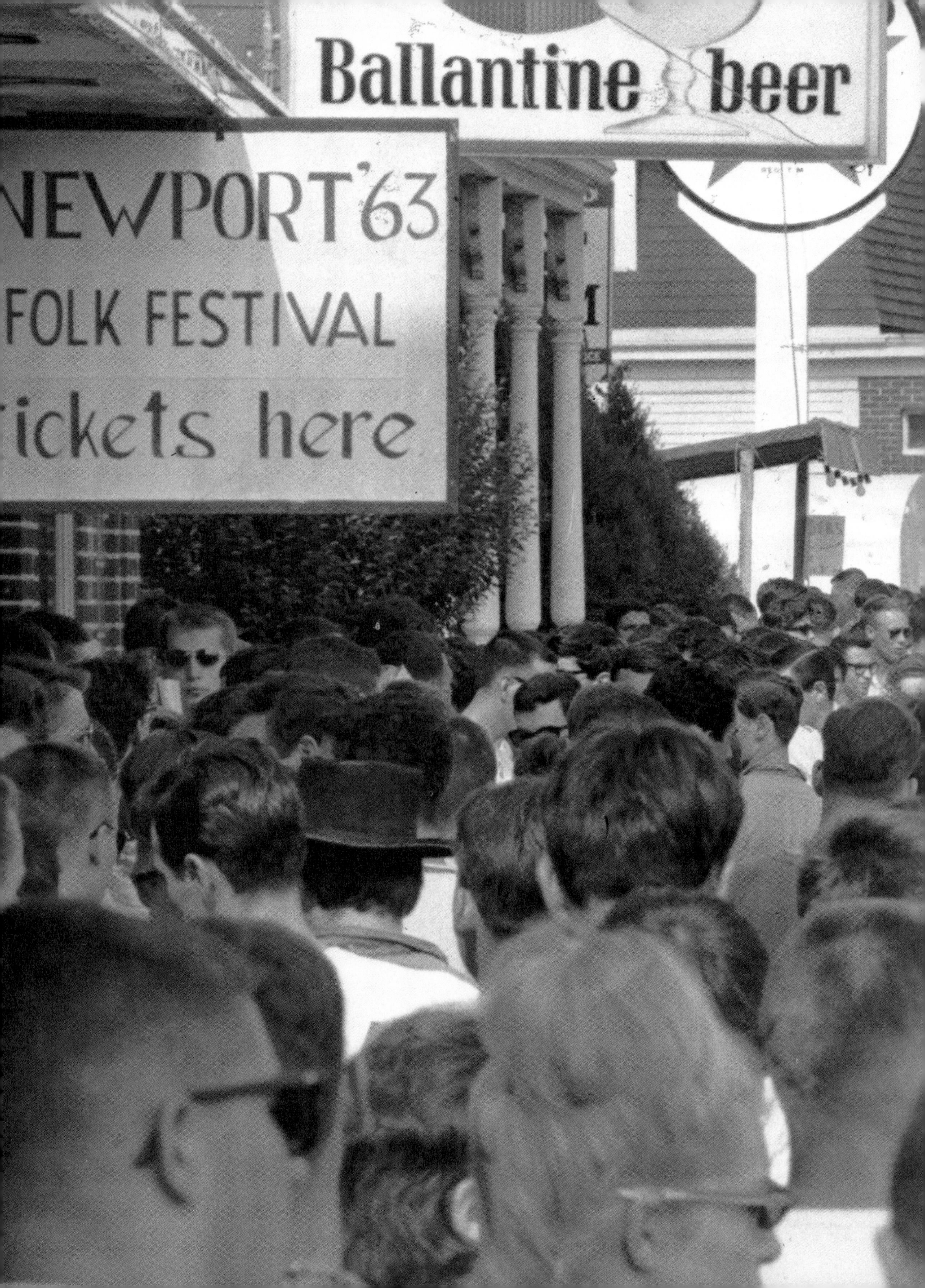
Ballantine beer
NEWPORT '63
FOLK FESTIVAL
ickets here

Onstage with Pete Seeger at Newport, 1963, and backstage with Joan Baez. Rumors about a romance between Joan and Bob were flying at the festival.

So Bob Dylan arrived in "New York town" in 1961 because, as he put it, "it was a great place for me to learn and to meet others who were on similar journeys." Some of these people were folksingers like Dave Van Ronk, Ramblin' Jack Elliott, Phil Ochs, Judy Collins, Pete Seeger, Tom Paxton, Barbara Dane, Paul Clayton and Mark Spoelstra. And it was to New York's Greenwich Village that he gravitated, where he not only found a thriving folk club scene at places like the Gaslight, Cafe Wha? and Gerde's Folk City but also wound up meeting and playing with such legendary blues musicians as John Lee Hooker and Big Joe Williams. Most important of all, Dylan finally got to meet and to become friends with his "last idol," Woody Guthrie—"for real" this time—who was slowly dying of Huntington's disease in nearby Morristown, New Jersey. Dylan wrote him a song " 'Bout a funny ol' world that's a-comin' along. / Seems sick an' it's hungry, it's tired an' it's torn, / It looks like it's a-dyin' an' it's hardly been born" ("Song to Woody").

It was a time when people put each other up for nights or weeks at a time and slept on friends' floors. And it was a time when one could live an exciting, adventurous life while being "decently poor." "Back then . . ." Dylan once recalled, "there wasn't any pressure. . . . You know, I mean, music people were like a bunch of cotton pickers. They see you on the side of the road picking cotton, but nobody stops to give a shit. I mean, it wasn't that important. So Washington Square was a place where people you knew or met congregated every Sunday and it was like a world of music. . . . There could be fifteen jug bands, five bluegrass bands and an old crummy string

An intense discussion with Joan Baez backstage at Newport in 1963. After the adulation they received at the festival, Joan invited Bob to appear, sometimes unannounced, at many of her subsequent concerts.

50

Dylan, coming and going, at Newport, 1963. Over the next three years, the Newport Folk Festival would be the showcase for changes in Dylan's music and philosophy, culminating in 1965 when his appearance with an electric guitar was greeted with derision.

band, twenty Irish confederate groups, a Southern mountain band, folksingers of all kinds and colors singing John Henry work songs. . . . Bongo drums, conga drums, saxophone players, xylophone players, drummers of all nations and nationalities. Poets who would rant and rave from the statues. You know, those things don't happen anymore. But then that was what was happening. It was all street. Cafés would be open all night. It was a European thing that never really took off. It has never really been a part of this country. That is what New York was like when I got there." But, as Dylan added, "Mass communication killed it. It turned into one big carnival sideshow. That is what I sensed, and I got out of there when it was starting to happen. The atmosphere changed from one of creativity and isolation to one where the attention would be turned more to the show."

Before that happened, Dylan entered the scene and started practicing his craft, writing and singing songs about the "luckless, the abandoned an' forsaked," as he put it in "Chimes of Freedom." He condemned the Ku Klux Klan in "The Death of Emmett Till" and the John Birchites in "Talkin' John Birch Paranoid Blues." In "Masters of War" he damned the war makers. And in "Blowin' in the Wind," he created probably his most famous song, though Dylan once stated that he wrote that song just for himself and for a few of his friends. In fact, this antiracist, anti-nuclear-war anthem (covered by everybody from Peter, Paul and Mary to Trini Lopez) is, in its deepest sense, a subtle plea for awareness ("How many times must a man look up / Before he can see the sky? / Yes, 'n' how many ears must one man have / Before he can hear people cry?")

Dylan had the zeal and fervor of a biblical prophet, but he also had a sense of humor and irony ("Talking Bear Mountain Picnic Massacre Blues"); and one soon started to notice that he was beginning to write songs that saw the

Dylan performing for his fans at Newport, 1964. He once said that he wrote his songs for all the people who couldn't express what was inside themselves: "It ain't the melodies that're important, man, it's the words."

54

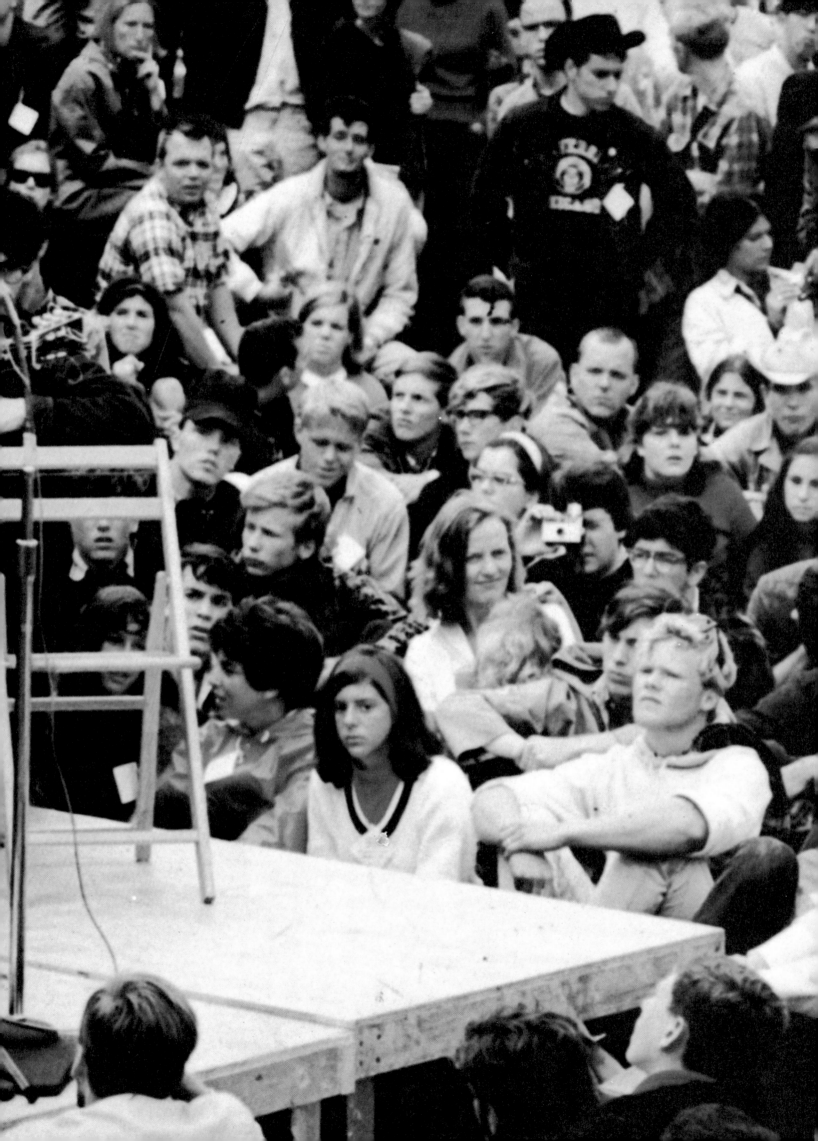

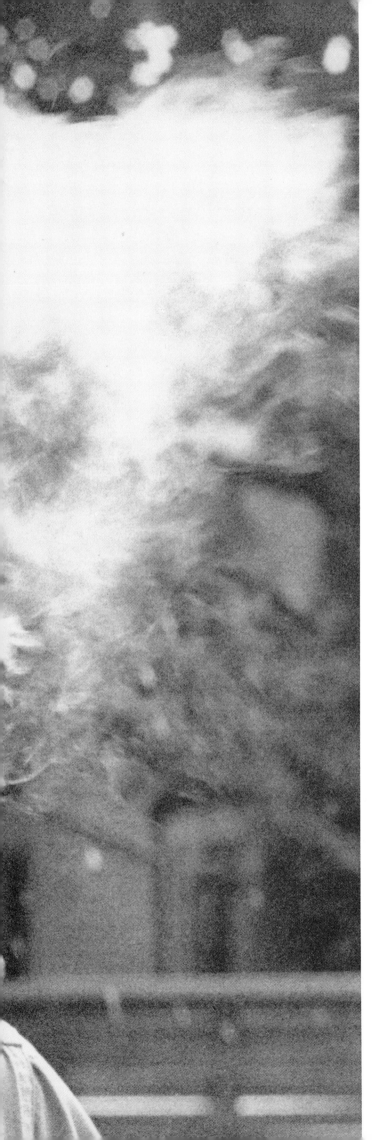

world as consisting not just of heroes and villains but of mostly cowardly people caught up in all-too-human situations. In a song like "Who Killed Davey Moore?" Dylan sings about the death of the boxer Davey Moore and dramatizes the excuses (in a way that echoes the rhyme "Who Killed Cock Robin?") given by the referee, the fighter's manager, the gamblers, the sportswriters and the crowd ("We just meant to see some sweat, / There ain't nothing wrong in that. / It wasn't us that made him fall. / No, you can't blame us at all"). And in "Only a Pawn in Their Game," Dylan suggests that the "poor white" killer of Medgar Evers was only the pawn of Southern sheriffs, politicians and the Social Lie ("He's taught in his school / From the start by the rule / That the laws are with him / To protect his white skin / To keep up his hate / So he never thinks straight / 'Bout the shape that he's in / But it ain't him to blame / He's only a pawn in their game"). Like Bertolt Brecht, Dylan wanted to make each member of his audience aware of *all* the elements in a situation and, in Brecht's words, "to leave him a changed man; or rather, to sow within him the seeds of changes which must be completed outside the theater." And again like Brecht, Dylan wanted to turn art "from a home of illusions to a home of experiences" in order to help people "master the world and [themselves]." (About Brecht, incidentally, Dylan once said, "He should be as widely known as Woody an' should be as widely read as Mickey Spillane an' as widely listened to as Eisenhower.") Dylan, too, wanted people to think and experience things for themselves. And when, for example, he sang about "the pellets of poison . . . flooding their waters" in "A Hard Rain's A-Gonna Fall," he said that he meant by that "all the lies that people are told on their radios and in the newspapers, trying to take people's brains away, all the lies I consider poison."

Early on, Dylan revealed one of his most persistent traits: any attempt to tie him down politically, musically or otherwise was bound

Dylan smoking a cigarette at Newport, 1963. After he gave up smoking, the timbre of his voice changed. That, he said, accounted for the relaxed way he sounded on Nashville Skyline.

Dylan practicing with his twenty-foot bullwhip outside the motel where the festival artists were staying.

58

to fail. "Greed and lust I can understand," he once stated, "but I can't understand the values of definition and confinement. Definition destroys. Besides, there's nothing definite in this world." Along with this notion was Dylan's refusal to repeat a song in exactly the same way. Early on in his career, when asked to play backup harmonica on a Harry Belafonte recording session, Dylan quit after playing on only one number. "Over and over again," he complained to one of his friends about the session. "Who needs that? The same thing again and again. That ain't singin'." And later, for his first Columbia Records album, Dylan commented: "Mr. Hammond* asked me if I wanted to sing any of them over again and I said no. I can't see myself singing the same song twice in a row. That's terrible." (As he was later to sing, "I ain't gonna work on Maggie's farm no more.")

Just as Hermes was Dylan's tutelary god, so, too, in an important way was Proteus, the Greek sea deity who had the power to change his form at will. And only when he was caught and bound—before he had time to elude his

Dylan relaxing at the motel pool in Newport, 1963. Above: Clowning with bassist Bill Lee: "Now Bob, can't you read? Registered guests only!" Right: Dylan showing off his invisible guitar to an invisible friend.

*John Hammond, who had recorded everybody from Bessie Smith to Pete Seeger, had signed up Dylan and produced his first album, *Bob Dylan*, for Columbia Records in 1961.

pursuers by a rapid change in shape, from dragon to lion to fire to flood—would he begin to make prophecies about the future. In the early Sixties, some of Dylan's friends had begun to take note of his uncanny ability to change his appearance almost from day to day. As Eric ("Ric") von Schmidt commented in 1961: "At this time Bob had the most incredible way of changing shape, changing size, changing looks. The whole time he was [in London] he wore the same thing, his brown jacket, blue jeans and cap. And sometimes he would look big and muscular and the next day he'd look like a little gnome, and one day he'd be kind of handsome and virile and the following day he'd look like a thirteen-year-old child. It was really strange. . . . You'd never know what he was going to look like."

And along with this changing appearance came the radically changed type of love song that he began to sing in the early Sixties —songs that broke the stereotyped mold of the boy-pleads-for-girl-for-ever-and-ever lyric. Dylan's idea was to send the girl brazenly and straightforwardly on her way ("It Ain't Me, Babe," "All I Really Want to Do," "Most Likely You Go Your Way"). In 1978 Dylan told an interviewer that when he had composed these earlier love songs, he was "writing more about objection, obsession or rejection." But out of these states and feelings Dylan created an art that in its supposed negativity in fact revealed an awareness of the illusions of possessive love ("You say you're lookin' for someone / Who will promise never to part, / Someone to close his eyes for you, / Someone to close his heart"—"It Ain't Me, Babe"; "I don't want to straight-face you / Race or chase you, track or trace you, / Or disgrace you or displace you, / Or define you or confine you"—"All I Really Want to Do").

And just at the moment that Dylan had become identified as a "folk and protest artist," he slipped away, like Proteus, and began to sing:

Yes, my guard stood hard when abstract threats
Too noble to neglect
Deceived me into thinking

I had something to protect
Good and bad, I define these terms
Quite clear, no doubt, somehow.
Ah, but I was so much older then,
I'm younger than that now.

—"My Back Pages"

He *sounded* younger, too, "Everything passes, everything changes," he sang in "To Ramona"; and he ended "Restless Farewell" with the lines: "So I'll make my stand / And remain as I am / And bid farewell and not give a damn."

One of the other fascinating, if obvious, things about Bob Dylan's mercurial personality was the way the timbre of his voice would change from one record or period of his life to another—as if his voice, too, couldn't stand having just one, unvarying sound. When he first arrived in New York City, he was singing like a hillbilly with a voice that sounded "like a dog with his leg caught in barbed wire," as someone remarked at the time. And as years went by, Dylan's voice would veer from, in his words, "that thin . . . wild mercury sound . . . metallic and bright and gold" of *Blonde on Blonde* (1966) to the relaxed country sound, which he attributed to his having stopped smoking cigarettes, of *Nashville Skyline* (1969) to the pinched-up, hypertense sound of *Street-Legal* (1978). For Dylan's voice—unlike that of almost any other rock singer—inescapably and inevitably reflected, like a vocal Rorschach test, his continually changing inner emotional states. (It is also interesting that, as Dylan once mentioned to me, his favorite singer was the Egyptian Om Kalsoum—an enormous star throughout the Middle East

Summertime, 1963: Dylan takes a dive. Next page: On the last night of the Newport festival, Dylan was joined by (left to right) Peter, Paul and Mary, Joan Baez, the Freedom Singers and Pete Seeger in singing "We Shall Overcome."

before her death. And when I asked Dylan if he liked Sufi and dervish singing, he replied: "Yeah, that's where my singing really comes from . . . except that I sing in America. I've heard too much Leadbelly really to be too much influenced by the dervishes.")

But people wanted to tie him down. "Most people walking around," he told Nat Hentoff in 1964, "are tied down to something that doesn't let them really *speak*, so they just add their confusion to the mess. I mean, they have some kind of vested interest in the way things are now. . . . All I can do is show people who ask me questions how I live. All I can do is be me. I can't tell them how to change things, because there's only one way to change things, and that's to cut yourself off from all the chains. That's hard for most people to do." And when he appeared to accept the Tom Paine Award from the Emergency Civil Liberties Committee in December 1963, he shocked his audience. As he recalled the incident: "When I got up to make my speech, I couldn't say anything by that time but what was passing through my mind. They'd been talking about Kennedy being killed, and Bill Moore and Medgar Evers and the Buddhist monks in Vietnam being killed. I had to say something about Lee Oswald. I told them I'd read a lot of his feelings in the papers and I knew he was uptight. Said I'd been uptight, too, so I'd got a lot of his feelings. I saw a lot of myself in Oswald, I said, and I saw in him a lot of the times we're all living in. And, you know, they started booing. They looked at me like I was an animal. They actually thought I was saying it was a good thing Kennedy had been killed. That's how far out they are. I was talking about Oswald. And then I started talking about some friends of mine in Harlem—some of them junkies, all of them poor. And I said they need freedom as much as anybody else, and what's anybody doing for *them*? The chairman was kicking my leg under the table, and I told him: 'Get out of here.' Now, what I was supposed to be was a nice cat. I was supposed to say: 'I appreciate your award and I'm a great singer and I'm a great believer in liberals, and you buy my records and I'll support your cause.' But I didn't, and so I wasn't accepted that night. That's the cause of a lot of those chains I was talking about—people wanting to be accepted, people not wanting to be alone. But, after all, what is it to be alone? I've been alone sometimes in front of three thousand people. I was alone that night."

And when, in 1965, Dylan appeared onstage at the Newport Folk Festival and shortly thereafter at Forest Hills, *not* alone with his acoustic guitar and mouth harp but accompanied by electric guitar and backup musicians, many of his fans called him a traitor and sellout (he was in fact called "Judas" many times during his 1966 English tour with the Band)—not realizing that he was actually returning to the way he used to perform back at Hibbing High's Jacket Jambourie Talent Festival. (The audience at that performance had been affronted, too.) Most of Dylan's fans had also forgotten or never known about the singer's quickly released—just prior to *The Freewheelin' Bob Dylan*—and equally quickly withdrawn first single for Columbia Records: a rocker called "Mixed-Up Confusion," backed by guitar, bass, piano, string bass and drums. But when Dylan returned to the Newport stage alone with his acoustic guitar to sing "It's All Over Now, Baby Blue" ("Leave your stepping stones behind, something calls for you"), he really must have known what it felt like to be on his own. In addition, when Dylan performed his electric version of "Maggie's Farm" at Newport with members of the Paul Butterfield Blues Band, his mike's volume had been turned off and his voice didn't come through. As Eric von Schmidt, who had been sitting in the front press section, recalled: "Nobody in the press section was yelling bring back the old Bobby or get the acoustic guitar. That started with the people in the back, a misunderstanding about what we were shouting. They might not have started hollering

---

Mrs. Hattie Carroll, who was memorialized by Dylan in "The Lonesome Death of Hattie Carroll" after he read an account of her death. For bringing a drink too slowly, the fifty-one-year-old black barmaid had been beaten with a cane by one very drunk William Devereux Zanzinger, a twenty-four-year-old white tobacco farmer. The song was Dylan's favorite cut on The Times They Are A-Changin'.

The Lonesome Death Of Hattie Carroll

WORDS AND MUSIC BY BOB DYLAN

back there if they hadn't heard hollering from the front. They thought we were putting Bobby down, so they started putting him down, and it just built from there."

In the period from 1965 to 1966, Dylan's dress and appearance again changed, and he now seemed somehow more androgynous. As writers Nora Ephron and Susan Edmiston described him during a mid-1965 interview: "He was wearing a red-and-navy op-art shirt, a navy blazer and pointy high-heeled boots. His face, so sharp and harsh when translated through the media, was then infinitely soft and delicate. His hair was not bushy or electric or Afro; it was fine-spun soft froth like the foam of a wave. He looked like an underfed angel with a nose from the land of the Chosen People."

And during these two years, Dylan released three albums—*Bringing It All Back Home, Highway 61 Revisited* and *Blonde on Blonde*—that not only defined himself for his generation but also helped to reveal his generation to itself. It is important to recall that the mid-Sixties were a time of extraordinary counter-cultural ferment and subversiveness. Haight-Ashbury hippies, American and French radical students, anti–Vietnam War demonstrators, Black Panthers, Maoist militants, free-love anarchists, Hindu and Buddhist converts, apocalyptic ecologists, commune dwellers, the Weathermen (who, of course, took their title from "Subterranean Homesick Blues")—all found their focus and energy expressed in rock music, of which Bob Dylan was one of the most influential exemplars. Even

Preceding page, right: The March on Washington, August 28, 1963, where 200,000 demonstrators heard Martin Luther King, Jr., give his famous "I Have a Dream" speech. Left: With Joan Baez in front of the Lincoln Memorial. This page: With Pete Seeger. Dylan would join him in Greenwood, Mississippi, for a concert supporting black voter registration. Following pages: Scenes from Greenwood.

71

Buffalo, 1964: Joan Baez and Dylan were lovers at the time of their tour together. Maimudes is standing in the doorway.

though, throughout his career, he continually avoided the role of "shepherd" or "leader" ("It's never been my duty / To remake the world at large / Nor is it my intention / To sound a battle charge"—"Wedding Song"), people took from his songs his passion and perceptions and made them part of their lives. It was his words and music that inspired them. And indeed Dylan *did* change the course of rock music by enlarging the possibilities of its range and significance. As the critic Paul Nelson wrote about the second of Dylan's mid-Sixties albums (though he might as well have been speaking about all three of them): "With the advent of *Highway 61 Revisited* . . . Bob Dylan has exploded . . . the entire city folk music scene into the incredibly rich fields of modern poetry, literature and philosophy. That he did it with his own personal blend of a popular music style, rock & roll, is all the more joyful and remarkable."

I still remember the howls of outrage from many professors of literature when they heard of critic Ralph J. Gleason's remark that, in his opinion, Bob Dylan was America's greatest contemporary poet. (Dylan himself had once remarked: "You don't necessarily have to write to be a poet. Some people work in gas stations and they're poets. I don't call myself a poet because I don't like the word. I'm a trapeze artist.") But the West Coast poet and critic Kenneth Rexroth was one of several nonacademic writers who clearly understood Gleason's remark and who went on to explain the situation in a marvelous essay entitled "Back to the Sources of Literature": "Most people do not even notice what is happening in the art of poetry for the simple reason that it never occurs to them that what is happening is poetry. . . . As in the days before the city and the alphabet, poetry has become once again an art of direct communication, one person speaking or singing directly to others. Along with this change has come, in the words of the poems themselves, a constant, relentless, thoroughgoing criticism of all the values of indus-

Scenes from the mid-Sixties: Above, Dylan salutes and makes it an act of defiance. At right, a poster store, where Dylan's salute appears among images of other heroes and victims of the times.

Dylan scowling on a park bench in Sheridan Square, 1965. He was then working on his fifth album, Bringing It All Back Home.

81

trial, commercial civilization. Poetry today is people poetry as it was in tribal society and it performs the same function in a worldwide counterculture. It is the most important single factor in the unity of that counterculture and takes the place of ideologies and constitutions, even of religious principles. As such, those whose lives are identified past recall with the older dominant culture are justified in seeing it as profoundly subversive. Where is this poetry? It is in the lyrics of rock singers, protest singers, folksingers, and the singers of gathering places like the French *cafés chantants* now spread all over the world." The roots of this poetry, of course, went back to the troubadours, *Carmina Burana* (the large collection of medieval student songs of love and protest), and François Villon, whom Rexroth calls "the poet laureate of five hundred years of the counterculture."* And Dylan himself acknowledged this tradition and extended it to our day in one of his *11 Outlined Epitaphs:*

with the sounds of François Villon
echoin' through my mad streets
as I stumble on lost cigars
of Bertolt Brecht
an' empty bottles
of Brendan Behan
the hypnotic words
of A. L. Lloyd
each one bendin' like its own song. . . .
the cries of Charles Aznavour
with melodies of Yevtushenko
through the quiet fire of Miles Davis
above the bells of William Blake
an' beat visions of Johnny Cash
an' the saintliness of Pete Seeger. . . .
it's all endless
an' it's all songs
it's just one big world of songs

As far as "exploding this folk-music scene into philosophy" was concerned, Dylan told the journalist Joseph Haas in 1965: "Philosophy can't give me anything that I don't already have. The biggest thing of all, that encompasses it all, is kept back in this country. It's an old Chinese philosophy and religion. . . . There is a book called the *I Ching,* I'm not trying to push it . . . but it's the only thing that is amazingly true, period, not just for me. . . . You don't have to believe in anything to read it, because besides being a great book to believe in, it's also very fantastic poetry."

"Change: that is the unchangeable" is the paradoxical notion of the *I Ching;* and connected with this notion is the belief in the essential relativity of Yin and Yang. Compare Dylan's "My love she speaks like silence, / Without ideals or violence, / She doesn't have to say she's faithful, / Yet she's true, like ice, like fire" ("Love Minus Zero / No Limit") to the Chinese sage Lao Tzu's "When everyone recognizes beauty as beautiful, / There is already ugliness; / When everyone recognizes goodness as good, / There is already evil," and one can readily perceive the connection. And strangely, Dylan's "philosophy" is also uncannily similar to that of the sixteenth-century Chinese philosopher Li Chih, who has been called the "greatest heretic and iconoclast in China's history." In his essay "Childlike Mind," Li had this to say: "Once people's minds have been given over to received opinions and moral principles, what they have to say is all about these things, and not what would naturally come from their childlike

---

*Some of the *Carmina Burana,* for example, sound like thirteenth-century Bob Dylan:

Right and wrong they go about
  Cheek by jowl together.
Lavishness can't keep in step
  Avarice his brother. . . .
If any cannot carry
  His liquor as he should,
Let him no longer tarry,
  No place here for the prude.
No room among the happy
  For modesty.
A fashion only fit for clowns,
  Sobriety. . . .

O truth of Christ,
O most dear rarity,
O most rare Charity,
Where dwell'st thou now?
In the valley of Vision?
On Pharoah's throne?
On high with Nero?
With Timon alone?
In the bulrush ark
Where Moses wept?
Or in Rome's high places
With lightning swept?

—Translated by Helen Waddell

And some of Dylan's sentiments echo the words of the fifteenth-century poet François Villon:

It's hard times as they say
and Christmas is a dead season. . . .
It's cold out there; for myself, though, strangely
the desire is greater to break out
of this space I inhabit in love's dungeon,
though the downpour puts a damper on my soul,
and there are a lot of bastards out there.

—Translated by Jean Calais

minds. No matter how clever the words, what have they to do with oneself? What else can there be but phony men speaking phony words, doing phony things, writing phony writings? Once the men become phonies, everything becomes phony. Thereafter if one speaks phony talk to the phonies, the phonies are pleased; and if one does phony things as the phonies do, the phonies are pleased; and if one discourses with the phonies through phony writings, the phonies are pleased. Everything is phony, and everyone is pleased." And this is simply Bob Dylan set in prose: "Obscenity, who really cares / Propaganda, all is phony"—"It's Alright, Ma (I'm Only Bleeding)."

In the three albums he released between 1965 and 1966, moreover, Dylan mercilessly put down everything he saw as phony, deadening and lifeless: "guilty undertakers," "drunken politicians," people who lived in "vaults" and who depended on "useless and pointless information," critics like the Mr. Joneses of the world, debutantes who knew what you needed but not what you *wanted*. When in the song "I Want You" he sang: "Now all my fathers, they've gone down, / True love they've been without it. / But all their daughters put me down / 'Cause I don't think about it," Dylan was suggesting that real desire is stronger than frustration or guilt. As he wrote in *11 Outlined Epitaphs:*

desire . . . never fearful
finally faithful
it will guide me well
across all bridges
inside all tunnels
never failin' . . .

I have read excellent and convincing psychological, philosophical, sociological, literary, cabalistic and other spiritual interpretations of Dylan's lyrics. Yet the one thing to

Dylan was fond of telling people that he'd run away from home and, in one version, that he'd worked as a carnival hand. Other times, he'd claim to be an orphan—after all, as "Bob Dylan" he had no parents.

Preceding page: Shooting pool and, this page, playing chess with Victor Maimudes and a friend in Woodstock, 1965.

Shopping in an Army-Navy store. Dylan's words weren't all that his fans adopted as their own. His vagabond clothes were imitated as well.

*Dylan driving around
Philadelphia at the time of his
Town Hall concert there,
November 1964.*

Woodstock: In the early Sixties, Dylan often stayed at manager Albert Grossman's home upstate when he needed to get away. Later on, when he had married Sara Lowndes, he bought his own place there. After his motorcycle accident, Woodstock is where he stayed, recuperating and rethinking his life.

remember is that, before they are anything else, Dylan's songs begin as the free and open expression of an unprogrammed and unconditioned artist—with Li Chih's "childlike" mind—exploring his own deepest perceptions about himself and the world ("I'm ready to go anywhere, I'm ready for to fade / Into my own parade, cast your dancing spell my way, / I promise to go under it"—"Mr. Tambourine Man") and coming back to have them confirmed by a generation of young people trying to find its way in the midst of social and personal unrest. As the novelist John Clellon Holmes then commented about Dylan: "He has the authentic mark of the bard on him, and I think it's safe to say that no one, years hence, will be able to understand just what it was like to live in this time without attending to what this astonishingly gifted young man has already achieved." Dylan's songs from the mid-Sixties, moreover, are as powerful and relevant today as when they were written:

Ah get born, keep warm
Short pants, romance, learn to dance
Get dressed, get blessed
Try to be a success
Please her, please him, buy gifts
Don't steal, don't lift
Twenty years of schoolin'
And they put you on the day shift
　　　　　—"Subterranean Homesick Blues"

Advertising signs that con you
Into thinking you're the one
That can do what's never been done
That can win what's never been won
Meanwhile life outside goes on
All around you. . .

96

For them that must obey authority
That they do not respect in any degree
Who despise their jobs, their destinies
Speak jealously of them that are free
Cultivate their flowers to be
Nothing more than something
They invest in. . . .
　　　　　—"It's Alright, Ma (I'm Only Bleeding)"

How does it feel
To be on your own
With no direction home
Like a complete unknown
Like a rolling stone?
　　　　　　　　—"Like a Rolling Stone"

"Chaos is a friend of mine," Dylan said during this period. And he unhesitatingly entered the world of Chaos—his Desolation Row, his Juarez, his Mobile. In more romantic terms, Dylan was following the poet Arthur Rimbaud's advice about becoming a *seer.* Rimbaud wrote: "The Poet makes himself a *seer* by a long, immense and reasoned process of *disordering the rules of all the senses.* All the forms of love, suffering, madness; he personally seeks out and exhausts in himself all the poisons, to save and keep only their quintessences." And it is hardly a secret that during this period, Dylan was experimenting with drugs. "They just bend your mind a little," he stated in *Playboy* in 1966, and added: "I think *everybody's* mind should be bent once in a while."

In "Subterranean Homesick Blues," Dylan was "mixing up the medicine," and in songs like "Just Like Tom Thumb's Blues" and "Stuck Inside of Mobile with the Memphis Blues Again" he upped the dosage and described the scene and the results: "Now the rainman gave me two cures, / Then he said, 'Jump right in.' / The one was Texas medicine, / The other was just railroad gin. / And like a fool I mixed them / And it strangled up my mind, / And now people just get uglier / And I have no sense of time."

And during this time when *everyone,* it seemed, was getting stoned, another, less an-

Reading the Herald Tribune *in Woodstock, 1964. During his early career, Dylan often would write songs suggested by news stories.*

Newport 1965: Shortly after his disappointing reception at the folk festival here, Dylan re-leased Highway 61 Revis-ited, *a collection of some of the greatest—and angriest—rock songs he has ever written.*

gelic, less ingratiating side of Dylan's personality seemed to emerge. Dylan's reported arrogance, aggressiveness, furtiveness and mistrustfulness (qualities that can be glimpsed in the film *Don't Look Back* and which, according to many of his friends and ex-friends, had always lain hidden beneath the surface of his personality) now exploded. His enormous fame and influence with their impossible demands, his mind-bending experiments with drugs, the difficulty he may have had handling his irrepressible and exigent perceptions and insights, his constant concertizing— all blocked Dylan's path of self-discovery, a path that demanded observation and attention and calmness and the time and space to be a light to oneself. In *11 Outlined Epitaphs* he had written:

"I'm happy enough now"
"why?"
"'cause I'm calmly lookin' outside an' watchin'
the night unwind"

But now it was *he* who was beginning to unwind. As he had written on the jacket notes to *Bringing It All Back Home:* "i accept chaos. i am not sure whether it accepts me." It didn't. And it was undoubtedly inevitable (and probably a blessing in disguise) that in 1966 he have a motorcycle accident, suffering several broken vertebrae, a concussion and lacerations of his face and scalp. For months on end he was forced to recuperate in the quiet of his Woodstock home with his wife, Sara Lowndes, whom he had secretly married in 1965, and his new family life.

"You gave me babies one, two, three / What is more you saved my life," Dylan sang in "Wedding Song." And in "If Not for You," he stated: "If not for you my sky would fall / Rain would gather too. / Without your love I'd be nowhere at all, / I'd be lost if not for you." And the evidence is irrefutable that Bob Dylan felt

Performing at the Newport Folk Festival, July 1965. Bringing It All Back Home *was selling thousands of copies a week, but Dylan had decided that he was going to play rock. When he marched onstage dressed in the Mod-style clothes he'd picked up in England, carrying an electric guitar, the crowd was dumbfounded. After a few songs, he relented and got out his acoustic.*

103

his life had been saved by his wife and the care that she provided him.

It might seem strange that this artist who had always insisted on the importance of doing things on one's own—and who entered the world of chaos, disconnection and fragmentation in order to explore it—*needed* someone so desperately. (As he sang in "Obviously Five Believers," "I guess I could make it without you / If I just didn't feel so alone.") One thinks of the incident Nat Hentoff mentions in his 1964 *New Yorker* profile in which Dylan, before beginning to record a song in the studio, signals to the producer and says, "I just want to light a cigarette so I can see it there while I'm singing," and adds, grinning: "I'm very neurotic. I need to be secure." Of course, this is hardly a moment that deserves too much psychological probing, but it does seem that Dylan always needed the loyal, if almost invisible, public presence of a woman who would allow him the freedom to function in his outer and inner worlds as he wished. As someone says to the character of Clara (Sara Dylan) in the film *Renaldo and Clara*, "I need you because I need your magic to protect me." Echo Helstrom, Suze Rotolo (who appears on the cover of *The Freewheelin' Bob Dylan* arm in arm with the singer, and who Dylan once called "the true fortune teller of my soul") and then Sara Lowndes had at one point seemed to fulfill this role. But now, Dylan was home from the seas, and he was serious about his role as a husband and father. As he sang in one of the songs of that time: "Strap yourself to the tree with roots / You ain't goin' nowhere."

During his long recuperation, he spoke to no one in the press. But in May 1967, Dylan broke his silence and told the *New York Daily News:* "What I've been doin' mostly is seein' only a few close friends, readin' little about the outside world, porin' over books by people you never heard of, thinkin' about where I'm goin', and why am I runnin', and am I mixed

Preceding pages: Dylan sparring with Donovan and Mary Travers at the Newport Folk Festival, 1965. At right: Talking things over with his manager, Albert Grossman, during the festival.

Dylan onstage at Newport with the Paul Butterfield Blues Band.

Dylan during a soundcheck at Forest Hills, August 27, 1965. His acoustic first set got a standing ovation; his electric set was booed by angry fans.

up too much, and what am I knowin', and what am I givin', and what am I takin'. And mainly what I've been doin' is workin' on gettin' better and makin' better music, which is what my life is all about." And early in 1968, he told *Newsweek:* "I used to think that myself and my songs were the same thing. But I don't believe that anymore. There's myself and there's my song, which I hope is everybody's song." Or, as the Chinese would put it, Dylan had gone from unwitting *identity* with the Tao to *knowing* the Tao, like passing from unconsciousness to consciousness, from a total reliance on intuition to a more distanced sense of control. He was now *writing* songs and not *living* them.

F rom 1967 to 1974, Dylan led a relatively quiet and undramatic life. According to Mrs. Beatty Zimmerman in her interview with Toby Thompson: "Bob goes to bed every night by nine, gets up in the morning at six and reads until ten, while his mind is still fresh. After that, the day varies; but *never* before. The kids are always around, climbing all over Bob's shoulders and bouncing to the music . . . they love the music, sleep right through the piano . . . and Jesse has his own harmonica, follows Bob in the woods with a little pad and pencil, jots things down . . . these are the things Bob feels are important . . . and this is the way he's chosen to live his life."

During these years, Dylan performed rarely in public (at the 1968 Woody Guthrie Concert in New York City and on the Isle of Wight in 1969, for example), but he did release a number of albums: *John Wesley Harding* (1968), *Nashville Skyline* (1969), *Self Portrait* (June

Preceding page: Dylan ironing Joan Baez's hair during their tour in 1965. Their love affair ended along with the tour, and it would be ten years before they sang together again. Left: With Robbie Robertson, Michael McClure, Allen Ginsberg and Lawrence Ferlinghetti.

1970), *New Morning* (October 1970), *Pat Garrett & Billy the Kid* (1973). (A two-record set of the incomplete *Basement Tapes,* recorded during this time, was eventually released in 1975.) And suddenly, from some quarters, Dylan started being attacked for his supposedly feckless and ascetic withdrawal from the ecstasies and inspired vertigo of his *Blonde on Blonde* creations. Simply, Dylan had reduced the allusiveness and complexities of his instrumental and verbal palette in records that were now about getting rooted and being happy instead of having continually to wander down that hard-travelin' road all alone. But for those who saw Dylan as an eternal rebel and wanderer, he seemed to have sold out. As Country Joe McDonald remarked somewhat uncharitably: "His mark of distinction was his intensity and funkiness. And when he was really on, it didn't matter that he couldn't sing or play—he was so present. Now he's like a ghost of his former self, and it drives me up the wall. I don't know where the real Bob Dylan went, but I don't believe this one, I haven't since *Nashville Skyline.* I don't know what happened to him, but something did—and he disappeared. He stopped being a rebel and started being a nice guy, a family man. He don't fool me, man."

In hindsight, however, it is clear that several of these albums contain some of Dylan's finest work. *John Wesley Harding,* in particular, is an extraordinary record that is filled with "legend, myth, bible and ghosts," as Dylan once described what folk music meant to him . . . and dreams, he might have added. For it is one of the first albums in which he presents two characters in his songs who, in some way, seem to represent two different parts of his personality needing and looking to be reconciled (the Joker and the Thief in "All Along the Watchtower" and Frankie Lee and Judas Priest in "The Ballad of Frankie Lee and Judas Priest"—the latter a song whose "moral" contains three of the wisest things Dylan ever

Preceding page: Julius and Peter Orlovsky, Robbie Robertson and Dylan at the Beats' landmark City Lights Bookstore in San Francisco. This page: With Andy Warhol and poet Gerard Malanga at the Factory, a New York scene. Warhol once gave Dylan a painting, which he traded to Grossman for a sofa.

119

wrote: "One should never be / Where one does not belong. / So when you see your neighbor carryin' somethin', / Help him with his load, / And don't go mistaking Paradise / For that home across the road").

The album also contained two country love songs—"Down Along the Cove" and "I'll Be Your Baby Tonight"—that pointed to the direction of *Nashville Skyline*. And here Dylan, on the album cover, greeted us with a face open and smiling to the world, and, on the record, with a light-textured voice that sounded like Roy Orbison or Elvis Presley singing "You're a Heartbreaker." After all, this was Dylan returning to his first musical love, country music (Hank Williams had been his first idol), and the album presented us with at least two magnificent songs—"Lay Lady Lay" and "I Threw It All Away"—the latter of which suggested, as John Lennon was to do soon thereafter, that love was indeed the answer (as, echoing Dante, Dylan sang, "Love is all there is, / It makes the world go 'round").

But his greatest works of this reflective period were the legendary, often bootlegged Basement Tapes—material cut by Dylan and the Band during his recording silence between *Blonde on Blonde* (1966) and *John Wesley Harding* (1968). Partially released commercially in 1975, these records contain both ebullient, deeply folk-rooted, quasi-nonsense songs like "Don't Ya Tell Henry," "Million Dollar Bash" and "Please, Mrs. Henry," and extraordinary meditations on memory and mortality in songs like "Tears of Rage," "This Wheel's on Fire," "Too Much of Nothing," "You Ain't Goin' Nowhere"—all filled with a haunted sense of the apocalypse and of the need for salvation and redemption. (It's interesting that among the numbers not included on the released album was the eerily prophetic "Sign on the Cross," which contains the spoken lines: "Ev'ry day, ev'ry night, see the sign on the cross just layin' up on top of the hill. Yes, we thought it might have disappeared long ago, but I'm here to tell you, friends, that I'm afraid it's lyin' there still. Yes, just a little time is all you need. . . .") One should also not slight the *Pat Garrett & Billy the Kid* soundtrack

album of 1973, which people took to be a throwaway record (except for the popular "Knockin' on Heaven's Door"), but which is actually a kind of beautiful, rough-hewn, mostly instrumental mantra album from the mythical Old West.

The much-reviled *Self Portrait* (mostly undistinguished versions of other people's songs) revealed a crisis in Dylan's music making; for an album to refer to the self and offer almost no sign of it was at best paradoxical, if not worrisome. *Self Portrait*'s title is ironical in the extreme, revealing, as it does, a portrait of someone fading into mostly borrowed songs whose words—in the saying of a great teacher—"are only like a window that has no light of its own, but only shines forth out of the light that it admits." Although *Self Portrait* found an audience that just liked the tunes, it's worth noting that the album was considered by some adepts to be an arcane and esoteric document, exemplifying, in one critic's words, a kind of "Eastern egolessness."

New Morning, which came out in October of 1970, provided more energy and definition of personality, especially with songs like "Went to See the Gypsy" and "Father of the Night." But it was not enough to satisfy Dylan's nemesis, A. J. Weberman, self-styled Dylanologist and Minister of Defense of the Dylan Liberation Front. Weberman appeared at Dylan's MacDougal Street doorstep in Greenwich Village, where he had moved during the summer of 1969—actually *in* and around his garbage bins, to be exact, since Weberman had decided that Dylan had become a sellout–capitalist pig who had turned his back on "the Revolution," and that an examination of Dylan's garbage would confirm this.

For his part, Dylan had often said that he had "always considered politics just part of the illusion" and had, furthermore, accepted the ancient Chinese idea that the notion of progress is alien to the concept of change. And earlier on, in *11 Outlined Epitaphs*, he had written: "there is no right wing / or left wing . . .

there is only up wing / an' down wing." But because of the often radical perceptions in his songs and almost in spite of himself, Dylan had become a political figure to the counter-culture, which took him to be, rightly I think, one of the important anarchist artists of the day. So Weberman, obsessed, took up his post at the singer's New York City garbage bins, searching for incriminating evidence of the "sellout." (Little did Dylan suspect when, years before, he had written the lines that would prophetically describe this situation perfectly: "The vagabond who's rapping at your door / Is standing in the clothes that you once wore" —"It's All Over Now, Baby Blue.") So, in 1971, Dylan decided to act and invited Weberman into his home, trying half-jokingly to do almost anything to get him out of his garbage. Weberman describes the scene: "We walked into his room filled with the band's instruments and D's paintings. They were these im-

pressionistic abysslike things. 'What do you think of my paintings?' 'Stick to poetry.' 'I paint what's on my mind.' 'Yeah, empty.' For the first time D laughed—IT TAKES A LOT to make Dylan LAUGH—but he could relate to emptiness. Then I decided to lay it on the line—'Dylan, you've got to live up to your responsibility as a culture hero—you're DYLAN, man, every freak has a soft spot in their heart for ya, they love ya, you're DYLAN, DYLAN, DYLAN.' 'I'm not Dylan, you're Dylan.' " "I'm not a myth to myself," Dylan had said, "only to others." But he was now expected to live up to the mythical character he had created.

In an especially candid moment during the interview we were doing for *Rolling Stone* in 1978, he told me about the creative problems he had encountered since the time he recorded *Blonde on Blonde*, twelve years before: "Right through the time of *Blonde on Blonde* I

A still from Don't Look Back. *Although Dylan would later disavow the film and complain that he never got a cent for it while the producers got rich, it remains a valuable record of his last acoustic performances.*

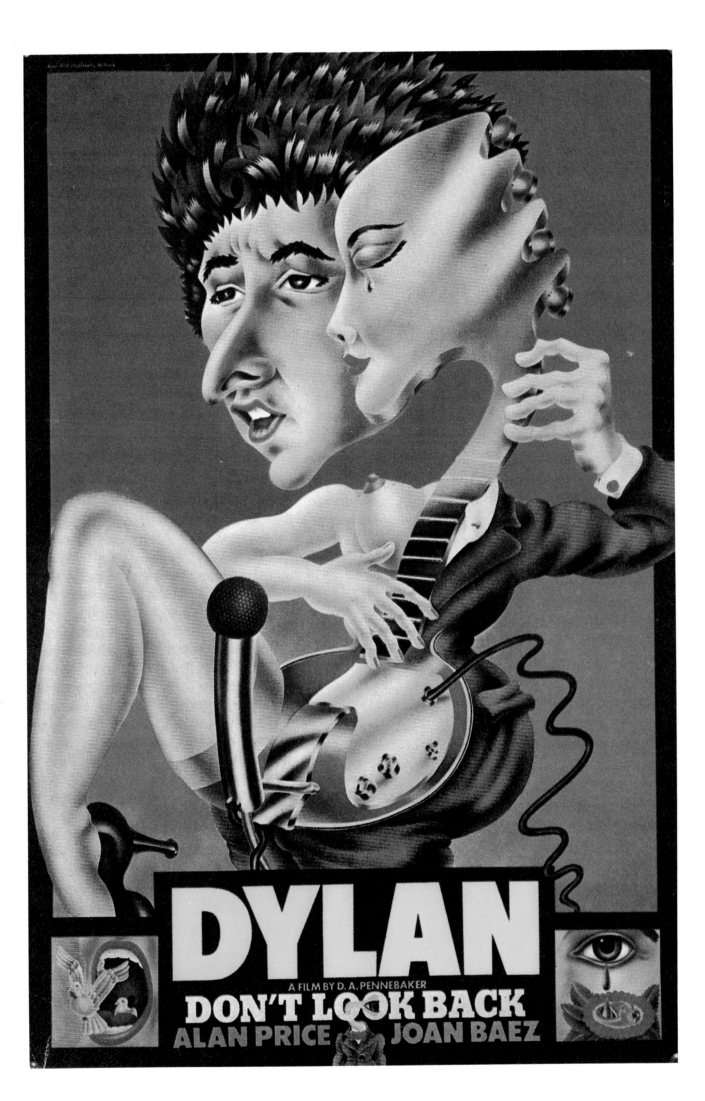

was [writing songs] unconsciously. Then one day I was half-stepping, and the lights went out. And since that point, I more or less had amnesia. Now, you can take that statement as literally or metaphysically as you need to, but that's what happened to me. It took me a long time to get to do consciously what I used to be able to do unconsciously.

"It happens to everybody. Think about the periods when people don't do anything, or they lose it and have to regain it, or lose it and gain something else. So it's taken me all this time, and the records I made along the way were like openers—trying to figure out whether it was this way or that way, just what *is* it, what's the simplest way I can tell the story and make this feeling real.

"So now I'm connected back, and I don't know how long I'll be there because I don't know how long I'm going to live. But what comes now is for real and from a place that's . . . I don't know, I don't care who else cares about it.

"*John Wesley Harding* was a fearful album—just dealing with fear [*laughing*], but dealing with the devil in a fearful way, almost. All I wanted to do was to get the words right. It was courageous to do it because I could have *not* done it, too. Anyway, on *Nashville Skyline* you had to read between the lines. I was trying to grasp something that would lead me on to where I thought I should be, and it didn't go nowhere—it just went down, down, down. I couldn't be anybody but myself, and at that point I didn't know it or want to know it.

"I was convinced I wasn't going to do anything else, and I had the good fortune to meet a man in New York City who taught me how to see. He put my mind and my hand and my eye together in a way that allowed me to do consciously what I unconsciously felt. And I didn't know how to pull it off. I wasn't sure it could be done in songs because I'd never written a song like that. But when I started doing it, the first album I made was *Blood on the Tracks*. Everybody agrees that that was pretty different, and what's different about it is that there's a code in the lyrics and also there's no

sense of time. There's no respect for it: you've got yesterday, today and tomorrow all in the same room, and there's very little you can't imagine not happening."

In 1974 Dylan separated from his wife, had a reconciliation with her in 1975, then got divorced in 1977. During these years, he frequently went out on the road, and produced a series of remarkable albums—*Planet Waves* (1974), *Blood on the Tracks* (1975), *Desire* (1975) and *Street-Legal* (1978). And in the song "Tangled Up in Blue" (from the second of these)—a song of longing for the vanishing beloved, as well as for the lost spirit of the Sixties—Dylan set the tone for these four albums, singing: "And when finally the bottom fell out / I became withdrawn / The only thing I knew how to do / Was to keep on keepin' on."

When we feel removed from the present, we can either remember and recollect the past or enter the spaces of memory where, as Dylan puts it, "there's very little you can't imagine not happening." In this regard, the psychologist Theodor Reik once concisely drew a distinction between remembrance and memory. "The function of remembrance," he wrote, "is the protection of impressions; memory aims at their disintegration."

Memory, of course, is deep within us—a place where things that are separate and cut off from our sense of the present always find a home. This is the world of the "night playing tricks when you're trying to be so quiet" ("Visions of Johanna"). And it is the world that belongs to the god Hermes where, in the words of Walter F. Otto, "Everything is equally far and near, close by us and yet mysteriously remote. Space loses its measures.

Portraits of Dylan in 1966. Preceding page: Smoking a cigarette and displaying his recently acquired wedding band; showing off his new Carnaby Street/Mod clothes; and (right) holding a crucifix. Dylan's mother says he was always interested in all religions.

Preceding page, left: Dylan at Hamlet's castle, Kronberg, Denmark, May 1966. Right: Arriving in Sweden from Australia with Maimudes. This page: Hamlet's cannons.

There are whispers and sounds, and we do not know where or what they are." It is a world of ghosts between things and of imaginary conversations with parts of the Self (as in "All Along the Watchtower" or "Isis"), a world in which what was asleep is now awake and what was once ordered and real is now disconnected and illusory: "All the people we used to know / They're an illusion to me now / Some are mathematicians / Some are carpenters' wives / Don't know how it all got started / I don't know what they're doin' with their lives" ("Tangled Up in Blue"). But just as the power of the negative bears witness to the positive, so the *awareness* of the illusory—discovered in rapturous and unsettling moments in the disintegrating world of memory—communicates nothing less than an ecstatic celebration of what is really real.

While memory provides many of the images and moods of "Something There Is About You" ("Rainy days on the Great Lakes / Walkin' the hills of old Duluth"), there is still a protective ambiguity in lines like: "I was in a whirlwind / Now I'm in some better place." More than any other song on the album—and it is a remarkable album—it is Dylan's seemingly throwaway "Never Say Goodbye" that glimmers with the timeless reality of rediscovered places, "Twilight on the frozen lake / North wind about to break / On footprints in the snow / Silence down below"—lines so reminiscent of old Chinese poetry.

Planet Waves has usually been spoken of as a collection of songs that specifically glorify Dylan's sense of family happiness. But there was an uneasy undercurrent flowing within the generally rhapsodic framework of this album. "Dirge" presented a half-bitter, half-pained threnody to a "painted face on a trip down suicide row" and to the singer's own feelings ("I hate myself for loving you and the weakness that it shows"), followed later by the self-justifying lines: "There are those who worship loneliness / I'm not one of them / . . . I've paid

With Françoise Hardy, a celebrated French pop singer. By the time of his 1966 European tour, Dylan had sold over 10 million records worldwide and had become an international sensation.

the price of solitude / But at least I'm out of debt." (Little did Dylan know how these words would come back to haunt him in *Blood on the Tracks*.)

And if "Dirge" was supposed to demonstrate the consciousness of bad faith, then the powerful "Wedding Song" revealed, as never before in Dylan's songs, the confusion of illusion and reality. For here is a love song in which Dylan affirms that he loves his wife more than time, love, madness, blood and even more than life itself. "Dirge" would be a more appropriate title for this song of death ("I'd sacrifice the world for you to watch my senses die"), for love is the law of life, and to love more than life is to negate both life and love, banishing them into an area of illusion and death. The wages of this attitude are the title of Dylan's *Blood on the Tracks,* as perfect an album as he has ever made.

"If your memory serves you well / You'll remember you're the one," Bob Dylan had sung in "This Wheel's on Fire." And when Dylan made his nationwide tour in 1974, his performances of older songs like "It's Alright, Ma . . ." and "Gates of Eden" must have reminded him of that person who, in writing those songs, had warned others not to become what he, in part—like many of us—had become. Now the songs themselves had become reminders and warnings to the soul: "How does it feel / To be without a home / Like a complete unknown / Like a rolling stone?" The audiences at Dylan's concerts sang out the chorus as if it were a national anthem. And what had once been an aggressive and admonitory sneer was now, in 1974, simply an invitation to reexplore a world that Dylan had turned his back on for many years.

"Shelter from the Storm" is a parable of the reuniting of two worlds that had been split apart in most of Dylan's songs since *John Wesley Harding*. Here, a formless, primordial creature of darkness, doom and rejection is embraced by a merciful, all-compassionate goddess / sister of unquestioning love: "Well

---

Throughout the tour of Europe Dylan was swarmed by fans and autograph seekers.

136

An illustration from Rock Dreams, *by Nik Cohn and Guy Peelaert, depicts Dylan's increasing loneliness and the isolation of superstardom.*

138

Paris, 1966: Dylan with Robbie Robertson, whom he had befriended the year before. At the time of this European tour, there was growing anti-American feeling on both sides of the Atlantic, and people were expecting Dylan to join in the criticism. Instead, he sought out the biggest American flag he could find to use as a backdrop at his shows.

I'm livin' in a foreign country / But I'm bound to cross the line / Beauty walks a razor's edge / Someday I'll make it mine."

It is this "foreign country" whose presence we feel in almost every song on *Blood on the Tracks*. It is a world of signals crossed and of times out of joint ("Shelter"), of soulmates losing their way and each other ("Simple Twist of Fate" and "If You See Her, Say Hello"), of love that betokens separation ("You're Gonna Make Me Lonesome When You Go"), of separation that betokens pain ("You're a Big Girl Now"), of the breath, no longer of life but of corruption and deceit ("Idiot Wind"), of barbed wire, hail and a never-rising sun ("Meet Me in the Morning"), and of a night journey in search of the beloved—"looking forever everywhere in hope of finding her somewhere," as the mystics say about the Eternal Beloved ("Tangled Up in Blue"). For it is clear that Dylan's separation from his wife set him back off on the road and "back in the rain," as he says in "You're a Big Girl Now." This is an image overflowing with associations from Dylan's older songs: "Lost in the Rain in Juarez" ("Just Like Tom Thumb's Blues") or "Nobody feels any pain / Tonight as I stand inside the rain" ("Just Like a Woman"). In Dylan's poetic world, "rain" is usually another word for "memory," where persons from the past and present and where love and pain reflect and merge with each other as in "buckets of rain / buckets of tears."

Considering the interflowing world of memory, it would, however, be mistaken for the listener to assign names and places to the songs on *Blood on the Tracks*. Dylan's fable "Lily, Rosemary and the Jack of Hearts," for example, presents a mirrored cabaret as the theater of the world in which you can see backstage women playing cards, a hanging judge, Lily and Rosemary, both of whom are in love with a diamond-mine tycoon ("in" on a bank robbery) who is soon to be stabbed to death by a jealous Rosemary, who winds up hanging on the gallows. Hovering over and around this scene is the Jack of Hearts—perhaps a playing card like all the others, an actor beyond compare (as the song informs us), and

a mysterious, almost transparent presence, whose power reveals as it conceals, much like Bob Dylan himself. This song, like many others, becomes a parable whose meaning must be worked out in each listener's head: "He moved across the mirrored room / 'Set it up for everyone,' he said / Then everyone commenced to do / What they were doin' before he turned their heads."

Arthur Rimbaud has always been an enormous influence on Dylan's imagery and sense of poetics. (A song like "Sad-Eyed Lady of the Lowlands," for example, "obliterates rational, introverted thought in poetry," as the critic Rosemary Tonks writes about Rimbaud, making "the word itself the equal of all concepts, and becomes them.") Here, in "You're Gonna Make Me Lonesome," Dylan more lightly sings about how his relationships have been like the one between Verlaine and Rimbaud (the "Foolish Virgin" meets the "Hellish Bridegroom" is how Rimbaud described the dramatic Verlaine and himself in *A Season in Hell*), concluding: "But there's no way I can compare / All those scenes to this affair / You're gonna make me lonesome when you go." This is Rimbaud filtered through the melody and gaiety of "I don't care if it rains or freezes / As long as I've got a plastic Jesus."

But the grace, lightness and humor of this song is as much a foil as is the poison and spleen of "Idiot Wind"—which exemplifies in Rimbaud's elegant phrase, "the refraction of grace crossed with a new violence." While "Idiot Wind" was the most obviously explosive and bitter work Dylan had released since "Positively Fourth Street" and "Can You Please Crawl Out Your Window?" it was also the first such song in which he incriminated not only the person he was singing about but himself as well: "We're idiots, babe / It's a wonder we can even feed ourselves."

Any emotion lived out in full, it has been said, is a form of love. And in "Idiot Wind," Dylan does nothing less than materialize a

---

Shortly after his European tour, Dylan suffered a near-fatal motorcycle crash and completely withdrew from the world. Secluded in his Woodstock home, he spent his recovery reading, writing music and painting. This self-portrait appeared on the October/November 1968 cover of Sing Out *magazine.*

SING OUT!
THE FOLK SONG MAGAZINE
VOLUME 18/NUMBER 4—OCTOBER/NOVEMBER, 1968—$1.00

EXCLUSIVE INTERVIEW WITH BOB DYLAN
INTERVIEW WITH BUKKA WHITE
TEN YEARS WITH THE RAMBLERS
WORDS & MUSIC TO "MR. BOJANGLES,"
"THE WEIGHT" AND OTHERS

Dylan enjoying the pastoral pleasures of Woodstock. He was leading the quiet life of a family man, just glad to be alive.

With the Band in front of Wild-Wood, a deserted house in Woodstock, 1968.

146

moment of wrath which, if not made visible and exorcised, will feed on the soul it destroys: "I kissed goodbye the howling beast / On the borderline which separated you from me"— while also seeing political evil as an extension of interpersonal hatred: "Idiot wind / Blowing like a circle around my skull / From the Grand Coulee Dam to the Capitol."

But while "Idiot Wind" is particularly searing, it is neither stronger nor weaker than any of the other songs on *Blood on the Tracks,* each of which has its own style—sometimes returning to previous periods of Dylan's career—its own setting and its own mood. And while each of the songs can be seen as just one of ten facets of Dylan's mind, each side of the album reveals a careful structural duplication of the other: each band is paired with its "double" on the other side: "Tangled Up in Blue" and "Meet Me in the Morning"—two songs of longing and ecstatic despair, "Simple Twist of Fate" and "Lily, Rosemary and the Jack of Hearts"—the first being a lover's dream of a city like Venice, the second a gambler's dream of a deck of cards; "You're a Big Girl Now" and "If You See Her, Say Hello"—the two most direct and poignant songs about rejection and the two least mediated by a narrative foil; "Idiot Wind" and "Shelter from the Storm"—songs that answer each other, in name and in spirit, as mercy tempers anger; and "You're Gonna Make Me Lonesome" and "Buckets of Rain"—both traditional in form, the first influenced by Buddy Holly and folk song, the second by Mississippi John Hurt, Mance Lipscomb and country blues. The result is a masterpiece.

Desire and *Street-Legal* mark Bob Dylan's re-emergence as a public personality. But between the release of these albums in 1975 and 1979, New Wave and especially disco music were taking over the radio and the clubs. As far as Dylan was concerned, most of what was going on was simply "programmed music" and "quadruple tracking" and "fictitious sound." As he was to say later in a different

Big Pink, the Band's house near Woodstock, where The Basement Tapes *were recorded. Next page: Dylan in the woods around Woodstock in his* John Wesley Harding *look, a somber note in a psychedelic time.*

*Dylan hanging out in front of
the Woodstock Bakery around
the time* Nashville Skyline
was released in 1969.

Dylan in a thoughtful moment, shortly before he was ready to emerge from his seclusion in Woodstock.

155

context: "[The music] has become soulless and commercial. Lot of it is played with drum machines and synthesizers. Personally, I'd rather hear an orchestra and a real drummer. Machines don't have the depth of the human heart. There just isn't anyone home." And as he stated it at that time: "There's no more rock & roll. It's an imitation, we can forget about that. Rock & roll has turned itself inside out. I never did do rock & roll. I'm just doing the same old thing I've always done." And while almost everyone else seemed to be frantically trying to push his or her way into Studio 54, Dylan, in the midst of his personal family crisis, formed the old-fashioned Rolling Thunder Revue—a kind of traveling hootenanny featuring lovers and friends from his past and present including Joan Baez, David Blue, Joni Mitchell, Roger McGuinn, Ramblin' Jack Elliott, Ronee Blakley, Bobby Neuwirth, Sam Shepard, Ronnie Hawkins, Allen Ginsberg and scores of other musicians, poets and hangers-on. And with this amazing group of personalities, Dylan wandered and performed around the country (Larry Sloman's book *On the Road with Bob Dylan* gives an exuberant account of the tour), all the while filming more than a hundred hours of the proceedings for what would turn out to be Dylan's four-hour movie, *Renaldo and Clara.*

The music in the film included songs from the *Desire* album. Released in December 1975, it became the singer's best-selling album to date—and featured the haunting "One More Cup of Coffee for the Road," a song about an outlaw and his fortune-telling wife and daughter, and two "protest" numbers (written in collaboration with Jacques Levy) about Dylan's notion of outlaw heroes—"Hurricane" Carter and Joey Gallo (two very strange bedfellows). But he was also singing two powerful songs—"Oh, Sister" and "Isis" (both also written with Levy)—addressed indirectly to his wife Sara, who appeared on the tour and who plays a leading role in the movie.

Writing songs at his piano, Woodstock, 1969. New Morning, *which was released in October 1970, was hailed not because it broke new ground but because it didn't. After the paradoxical* Self Portrait, *the old Dylan, it seemed, was back.*

Isis, the Egyptian earth goddess who was both wife and sister to her husband/brother Osiris, is, in Dylan's song, the estranged wife whom the mortal hero has to win back in a quest of endurance. Traveling east and north to a land filled with pyramids of ice (though it feels like the Mexico of Coronado) with a fortune hunter (who may be only another aspect or "double" of the hero himself), the hero fails to find the promised precious jewels but returns to try to win back his goddess wife:

She said, "Where ya been?" I said, "No place special."
She said, "You look different." I said, "Well, I guess."
She said, "You been gone." I said, "That's only natural."
She said, "You gonna stay?" I said, "If ya want me to, yes."

"Isis, oh Isis, you mystical child / What drives me to you is what drives me insane," the singer-hero cries out. And in the song "Sara"—also on *Desire*—Dylan directly addresses his wife by name, as he had never done on a record before (calling her "radiant jewel, mystical wife").

Dylan's three magnificent songs to his semiestranged wife, his dramatic re-creation of his love affair with Joan Baez, and his exploration of the secret of his own identity are all at the heart of *Renaldo and Clara,* in which, once and for all, Dylan consciously and playfully uses and examines the myth of "Bob Dylan." (In the film, "Bob Dylan" is played by Ronnie Hawkins, while Bob Dylan plays "Renaldo," Sara Dylan plays "Clara," and Joan Baez plays the "Woman in White.") "So Bob Dylan may or may not be in the film," I asked him in 1978. "Exactly," Dylan replied. "But Bob Dylan *made* the film," I responded. "Bob Dylan didn't make it. *I* made it," was his reply.

"*I* is another," wrote Arthur Rimbaud, and this statement is certainly demonstrated by *Renaldo and Clara,* in which characters in

Woodstock: George Harrison visited Dylan here in 1970. They got along well and collaborated on a song, "I'd Have You Anytime," which they recorded together.

The Woody Guthrie Memorial Concert at Carnegie Hall, 1968, Dylan's first public appearance after the accident. He and the Band performed three of Woody's songs.

161

Dylan appeared on the first show of Johnny Cash's TV series, 1969. Cash was one of Dylan's first important supporters, back in his early days at CBS in 1961.

163

The Isle of Wight Festival of Music
Woodside bay near Ryde _____ I.W
AUGUST 29·30·31st _____ season ticket £2·10

Present
Bob Dylan
the band & ritchie havens

masks and hats—often interchangeable—sit in restaurants and talk, disappear, reappear, exchange flowers, argue, visit cemeteries, play music and travel around in trains and vans. But a closer look will tell you that the film is actually about just one man—who could pass for the Jack of Hearts, the leading actor of "Lily, Rosemary and the Jack of Hearts," a card among cards, an image among images— and just one woman. Together they find themselves in the grip of a series of romantic encounters that seem to be reenactments of an occult ritual, culminating in the confrontation of the Woman in White, Clara and Renaldo— a meeting at the border of myth and reality. Using his physical image and name as the raw material of the film, Bob Dylan—like the Renaissance kings of masque and spectacle— moves daringly and ambiguously between fiction, representation, identification and participation.

Renaldo and Clara is, of course, a movie filled with magnificently shot and recorded concert footage of highly charged Dylan performances of songs like "It Ain't Me, Babe," "A Hard Rain's A-Gonna Fall" and "Knockin' on Heaven's Door"—the last of whose delicate and eerie instrumental breaks makes you feel as if you were entering paradise itself. Avoiding all of the pounding-and-zooming clichés of television rock & roll specials, the cameras either subtly choreograph the songs—revealing structures and feelings—or else look at the white-faced Dylan and the accompanying painted musicians in rapturous and intensely held close-ups.

Around these musical episodes, Dylan has woven a series of multilayered and multilevel scenes—unconsciously echoing similar moments in films by Cocteau, Cassavetes and Jacques Rivette—each of which lights up and casts light on all the others. Scenes and characters duplicate and mirror each other, are disassociated and recombined—all of them, in the words of the director, "filled with reason and not with logic." Thus, when Clara (Sara Dylan) says to Renaldo: "I am free . . . I can change," it brings back to us the words spoken earlier by Renaldo: "I haven't changed that much. Have you?" To which the Woman in White (Joan Baez) replies: "Maybe."

Renaldo and Clara is an ambitious, fascinating and illuminating movie. When I asked him what he thought the movie revealed, Dylan replied: "This film reveals that there's a whole lot to reveal beneath the surface of the soul, but it's unthinkable. . . . It reveals the depths that there are to reveal. And that's the most you can ask, because things are really very invisible. . . . And this film goes as far as we can to reveal that." And in an exchange with *Playboy* at that time, Dylan explained what he thought the film was about:

DYLAN: It's about the essence of man being alienated from himself and how, in order to free himself, to be reborn, he has to go outside himself. You can almost say that he dies in order to look at time and by strength of will can return to the same body. . . .

PLAYBOY: What are [Renaldo's] needs?

DYLAN: A good guitar and a dark street.

PLAYBOY: The guitar because he loves music, but why the dark street?

Above, left: A poster announcing Dylan's appearance at the Isle of Wight, August 1969. It was his first paid performance in four years, and though the event attracted 200,000 fans, many people were disappointed with the Dylan who showed up. His voice and his words had mellowed during his long absence, and he no longer seemed so angry.

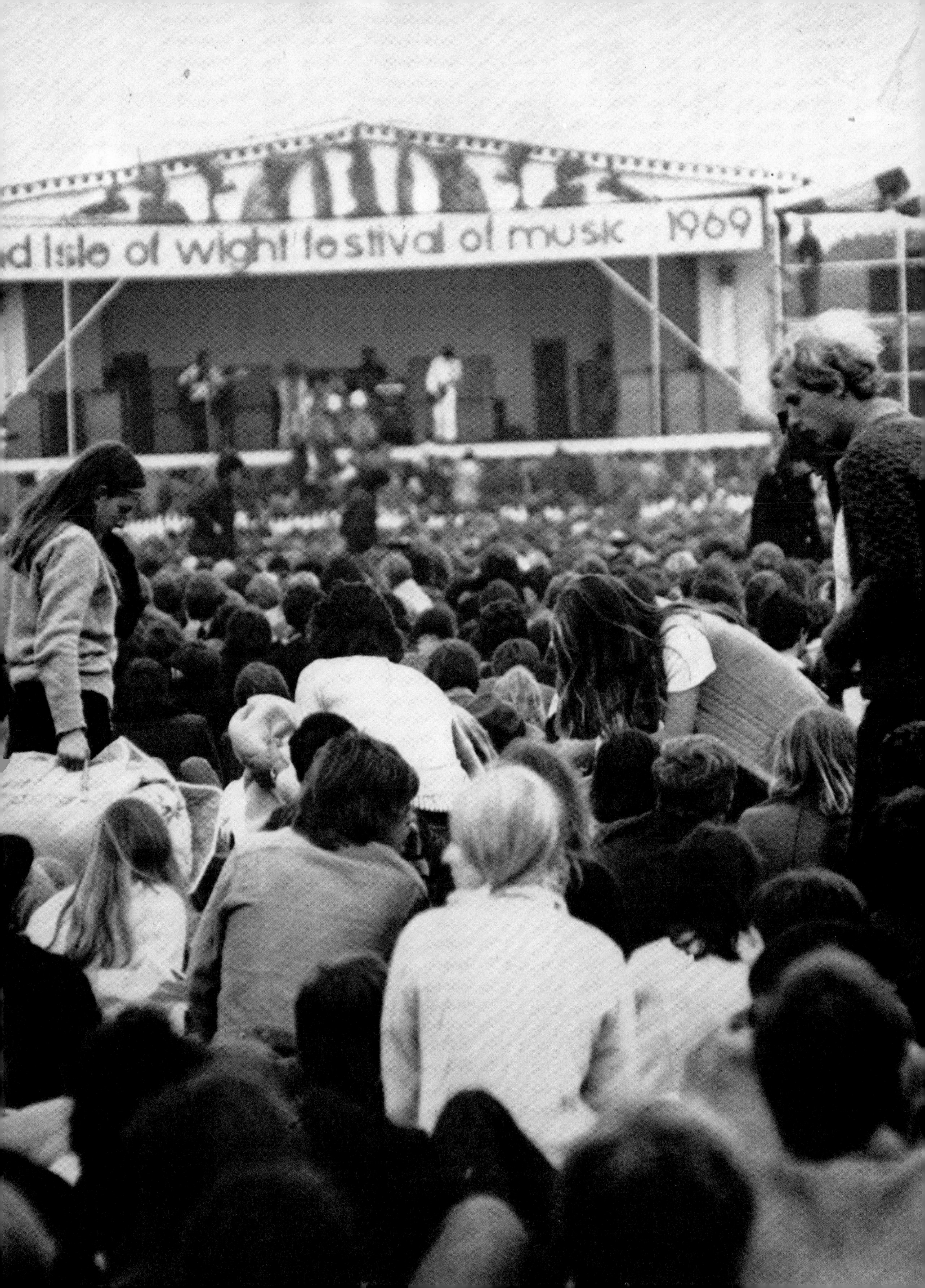
nd isle of wight festival of music 1969

The Isle of Wight Festival lasted two days, and many fans crowded into tents provided on the grounds. One tent bore the name "Desolation Row."

DYLAN: Because he needs to hide. . . . From the demon within. But what we all know is that you can't hide on a dark street from the demon within. . . . He tries to escape from the demon within, but he discovers that the demon is, in fact, a mirrored reflection of Renaldo himself.

In his book *Tarantula,* Dylan had earlier written his own epitaph:

Here lies bob dylan . . .
killed by a discarded Oedipus
who turned
around
to investigate a ghost
an' discovered that
the ghost too was more than one person.

Clearly, Dylan has always been obsessed with the problem of identity. In *Moby Dick,* Melville wrote about Narcissus, "who, because he could not grasp the tormenting, mild image he saw in the fountain, plunged into it and was drowned. But that same image we ourselves see in all rivers and oceans. It is the image of the ungraspable phantom of life; and this is the key to it all."

Robert Zimmerman had once said that he wished to be both "invisible" and "famous" and had gained a reflection of himself by fashioning the character of "Bob Dylan." His wife, too, was part of this reflection. But now his marriage had broken up, and *Renaldo and Clara*—upon which he had pinned his hopes of making more films in the future ("We're gonna make some movies that are gonna blow Hollywood apart," he had enthusiastically predicted to Larry Sloman)—had turned into an undeserved critical and commercial failure. Clearly, Bob Dylan's self-image was becoming increasingly shaky; and he seems to have been finding his identity fragmenting, with demons, phantoms and doubles threatening from within, his mask unable to protect him, with no place left to hide and no direction home.

In "Where Are You Tonight? (Journey Through Dark Heat)," the song that concludes *Street-Legal,* Dylan gives us an amaz-

ingly powerful depiction of personal disintegration of a man ineluctably in exile, trying desperately and futilely to hold on in a world where light and dark forces—both in the personality and in the cosmos—which were once partners in a harmonious creation, are now split and polarized and at war with each other:

There's a long distance train rolling through the
*   rain*
Tears on the letter I write
There's a woman I long to touch and I miss her so
*   much*
But she's drifting like a satellite. . . .

The truth was obscure, too profound and too pure
To live it you have to explode
In that last hour of need, we entirely agreed
Sacrifice was the code of the road. . . .

He took dead-center aim, but he missed just the same
She was waiting, putting flowers on the shelf
She could feel my despair as I climbed up her hair
And discovered her invisible self. . . .

I fought with my twin, that enemy within
Till both of us fell by the way
Horseplay and disease is killing me by degrees
While the law looks the other way. . . .

There's a white diamond gloom on the dark side of
*   this room*
And a pathway that leads up to the stars
If you don't believe there's a price for this sweet
*   paradise*
Remind me to show you the scars. . . .

This song, in fact, reminds me of the last work Van Gogh painted before his suicide, *Crows over the Wheat Field,* with what art critic Meyer Schapiro calls its "rapid convergences and dizzying angularities"—a work "unstable and charged with a tempestuous excitement." And what Schapiro writes about Van Gogh's painting might also be said about Dylan's song: "But the stable, familiar earth, interlocked with the paths, seems to resist perspective control. The artist's will is confused, the

In 1970, Dylan accepted an honorary doctoral degree from Robert Goheen, president of Princeton University. Throughout the Vietnam War, students were protesting military research on campus, and Dylan wore a white armband, showing support, in deference to his radical critics.

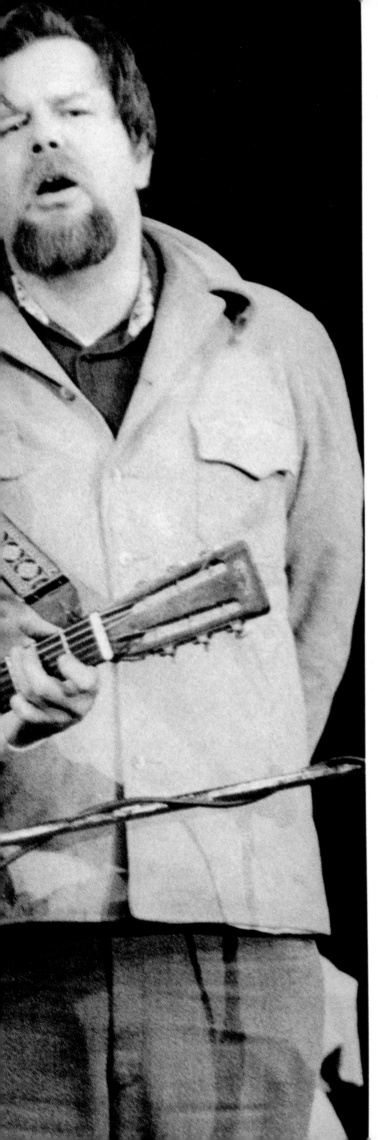

world moves towards him, he cannot move toward the world. It is as if he felt himself completely blocked, but also saw an ominous fate approaching."

Although *Street-Legal* contained some mysterious and gripping songs—"Changing of the Guards," "No Time to Think," "Señor (Tales of Yankee Power)"—it was critically maligned, especially by Dylan's veteran fans, as was, at least in America, Dylan's 1978 worldwide tour, which produced the *Bob Dylan at Budokan* double album, filled with mostly wonderful reworkings of Dylan's classic compositions. In former days, Dylan would have uncompromisingly moved ahead and paid the vituperative criticism little heed ("A hero," he once said, "is anyone who walks to his own drummer"). But as he now sang on his apocalyptic-sounding "Señor": "This place don't make sense to me no more / Can you tell me what we're waiting for, Señor?" He once told a reporter: "No man can fight another like the man who fights himself. Who could be a stronger enemy? . . . You can either do yourself in, or do yourself a favor. If you deal with the enemy within, then no enemy without can stand a chance." But the fight with the enemy within had taken a lot out of Dylan, and the enemy without was waiting for him. For several turbulent, troubled years Dylan had offered up his innocence and had gotten repaid with scorn. And he now desperately needed shelter from the storm, which came in the form of the sign of the cross and born-again Christianity.

Dylan recorded three albums during his born-again period—*Slow Train Coming, Saved* and *Shot of Love*—and on the third of these he gave us one of the deepest and most beautiful songs he ever wrote, "Every Grain of Sand," which simply describes the state he was in at that time:

Preceding page: Along with George Harrison and Leon Russell, Dylan performed at a benefit concert for the starving refugees of war-torn Bangladesh at Madison Square Garden in August 1971. This page: With Phil Ochs and Dave Von Ronk, at the 1974 Friends of Chile concert, held to raise funds for Chilean leftist prisoners. Dylan surprised many people by showing up at these two frankly political events. Next page: This photograph was intended to be the cover of Self Portrait, *but at the last minute Dylan replaced it with one of his own paintings.*

Dylan wrote the soundtrack for the Sam Peckinpah film Pat Garrett and Billy the Kid *and played an outlaw named Alias.*

179

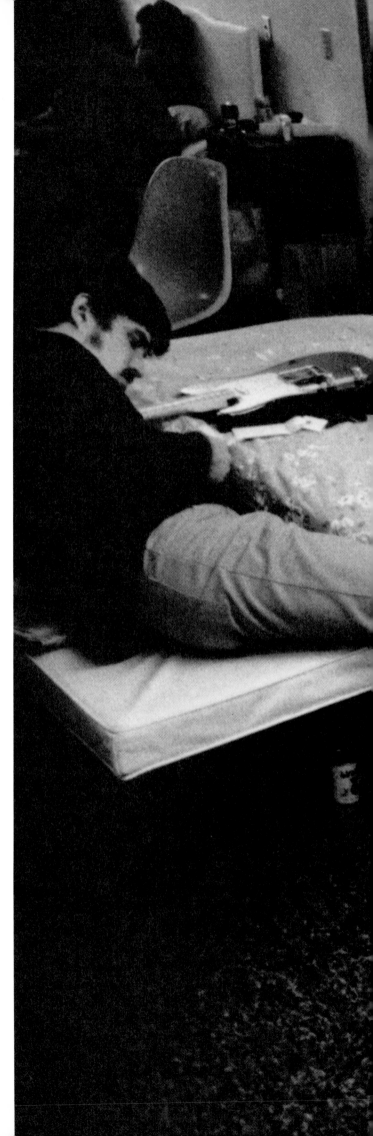

*In the time of my confession, in the hour of my deepest
    need,*
*when the pool of tears beneath my feet flood ev'ry new
    born seed,*
*there's a dyin' voice within me reaching out some-
    where*
toiling in the danger and in the morals of despair.
*Don't have the inclination to look back on any mis-
    take.*
*Like Cain, I now behold this chain of events that I
    must break.*
*In the fury of the moment I can see the Master's
    hand,*
in ev'ry leaf that trembles, in ev'ry grain of sand.

*On the flowers of indulgence and the weeds of yester-
    year,*
*like crim'nals they have choked the breath of con-
    science and good cheer.*
*The sun beat down upon the steps of time to light my
    way,*
to ease the pain of idleness and the memory of decay.
I gaze into the doorway of temptation's angry flame,
*and ev'ry time I pass that way I always hear my
    name.*
Then onward in my journey I come to understand
that ev'ry hair is numbered like ev'ry grain of sand.

*I have gone from rags to riches in the sorrow of the
    night,*
*in the violence of a summer's dream, in the chill of a
    wintery light,*
in the bitter dance of loneliness fading into space,
*in the broken mirror of innocence on each forgotten
    face.*
I hear the ancient footsteps like the motion of the sea.
*Sometimes I turn; there's someone there. Other times
    it's only me.*
I am hanging in the balance of the reality of man,
like every sparrow falling, like ev'ry grain of sand.

There is no dramatizing or haranguing or
polemicizing in this song—just the presenta-
tion of a sense of mystery and despair and

---

*The Band backstage. From the time of Dylan's motorcycle accident in 1966,
there had been rumors that he would tour with the Band. Dylan and his
buddies finally took to the road in January 1974, selling out arenas across the
country. Next page: The Band onstage.*

San Francisco, March 1975:
Dylan made a surprise
appearance at the SNACK
benefit concert—Students
Need Athletics, Culture and
Kicks. His wife Sara
watched from backstage.

*Performing at the SNACK
show with Neil Young.*

Autumn 1975: Dylan envisioned the Rolling Thunder Revue as an ensemble that would take a town by surprise, play a concert, and then disappear down the road, its itinerary a secret.

188

PALACE
ROLLING
THUNDER REVUE
BOB DYLAN
JOAN BAEZ
TUE NOV 11TH
RESTAURANT
HOTEL

(and *makes* public records) to argue his religious creed and to judge his listeners, it may not be inappropriate for a listener to make a public response.

To me, there is something extremely unsettling in the preprogrammed, puritanical and often propagandizing form of fundamentalist Christianity that Bob Dylan chose to purvey in his born-again songs. After all, this was the person who once declared: "People that march with slogans and things tend to make themselves a little too holy. It would be a drag if they, too, started using God as a weapon" (*Playboy*, 1966) and who was now singing: "There's a Man up on a cross / And He's been crucified for you. / Believe in His power. / That's about all you got to do" ("When You Gonna Wake Up?"); who once sang lovingly about a woman who "knows too much to argue or to judge," but who was now singing complaints about "adulterers in churches, / And pornography in the schools" ("When You Gonna Wake Up?"); who was making judgments about "my loved ones turning into puppets" ("Slow Train") and accusing those who didn't believe the way he believed of having "heart[s] of stone" ("Property of Jesus"); who was putting a new conditional twist on the Golden Rule in the song "Do Right to Me Baby (Do Unto Others)" when he sang: "But *if* you do right to me, baby, I'll do right to you, too" (emphasis added); and who, finally, in this same song admitted: "Don't wanna touch nobody, don't wanna be touched." As Paul Williams rightly asks in *Dylan—What Happened*, a book that is highly sympathetic to Dylan's born-again songs: "Dylan has said a great deal to us (and for us) over the years about politics and sexual love and the importance of being true to one's own vision. Does he now believe it's a sin to let another person see you naked? Does he believe the United States of America has God on its side? Does he feel comfortable with the idea that most of his fellow humans are eternally damned while he and a few oth-

awe, and the realization that the saving power can come at exactly the darkest hour—and it elicits from Dylan one of the most ethereal, healing harmonica solos he has ever presented on record.

In the songs from this period, Dylan tells us that he was broken and shattered, that the Lord rebuilt and filled him up, and that he was "saved by the blood of the lamb." In "Saving Grace" he says, "I've escaped death so many times, / I know I'm only living by the saving grace that's over me." One is grateful that Dylan overcame the negative forces that were leading him on to self-destruction and that he found the fellowship he needed among his born-again friends to start living a fulfilled life once again. But there are some questions that need to be asked.

Religion, someone once said, is what a person does with his or her aloneness. And as the sixteenth-century French philosopher Montaigne wisely wrote: "It is not for show that our soul shall play its role; it is with ourselves, inside, where no eyes can see but our own." It is, therefore, usually best to be reticent about discussing someone's personal religious beliefs. But when a person goes on public record

Spiritual descendants of Jack Kerouac and Neal Cassady, the Rolling Thunder Revue roamed the Northeast in chartered buses. Above: Dylan's room in one hotel on the tour. Right: Along with Jack Elliott and bassist Rob Stoner, Dylan backs a solo by his former costar Joan Baez.

Sunrise revel: a scene from Dylan's four-hour surrealistic epic, Renaldo and Clara, *filmed during the Rolling Thunder tour.*

*With Allen Ginsberg,
Dylan stopped in Lowell,
Massachusetts, to honor Jack
Kerouac, a writer who had
inspired him. The two recited
verses from "Mexico City
Blues" over Kerouac's grave.*

195

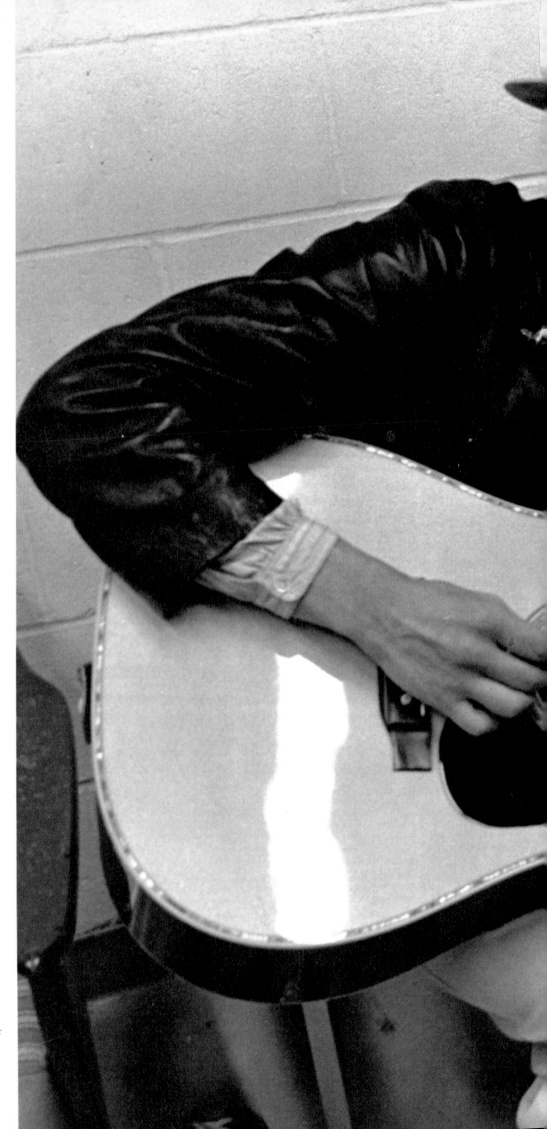

Preceding page: Bruce Springsteen, Mick Ronson, Ronee Blakley, Bob Neuwirth, Rob Stoner, Jack Elliott and Joni Mitchell backstage at a Rolling Thunder performance. Right: With Allen Ginsberg.

198

Most comfortable when shrouded in mystery, Dylan was masked or painted like a clown during the Rolling Thunder concerts.

201

ers are saved because they found the one true Faith? By refusing to sing his old songs, is he repudiating everything he once stood for?"

To give the devil (or should I say the *angel*?) his due, I should remind both myself and the reader that, as the Jungian analyst Jeffrey Satinover has written: "Once the star is established, his fans will tear him to pieces should ever he fail to carry for them the projected childhood Self. A recent example from pop culture is the fans' vituperative reaction to Bob Dylan's unexpected changes of style. Once a narcissistic complementation has been set up between any leader and his following, he is as bound as they. The rigidity of the relationship and the strength of the forces maintaining the status quo stem from the mutual common individual fear of fragmentation." Or as Dylan told the Minneapolis weekly *City Pages* in 1983: "People want to know where I'm at because they don't know where they're at."

It is true that throughout Dylan's career, so-called fans of his have given up on or disapproved of him at various stages of his musical and personal journey. And of course, many survivors of the Sixties and Seventies found themselves taking the path of one cult or sect or another in times of *their* insecurity and need,* and may have seen in Dylan's conversion a justification or some comfort for themselves. But Satinover also points out that true spiritual seekers attempt to go beyond a tenacious clinging-to-cults that simply provides some kind of easy and ultimately false sense of personal identity for themselves, and that they do not get "attracted to perfected, closed systems with guaranteed results. For such individuals, spirit and meaning are always great open questions; they are led onward by doubt

Among the duets Dylan and Baez performed at Rolling Thunder shows were "Mama, You Been on My Mind," a song she'd inspired a decade earlier, and his classic "The Times They Are A-Changin'."

*In the late Sixties, the psychiatrist Robert Jay Lifton interestingly pointed out that "a set of psychological patterns characteristic of contemporary life . . . are creating a new kind of man—a 'protean man.' " And Lifton defined "protean man" as one who changed allegiances and ideologies, often in rapid and contradictory succession, as a response to a breakdown of traditional images and values. And in a sense, Dylan's personality reflects this breakdown.

*Dylan at the side of the road:
"I won't join a group . . . .
When you fail in a group you
can blame each other. When
you fail alone, you yourself
fail."*

205

The ever-elusive Dylan hides in the doorway of a mime studio. He was always transforming himself, and he rarely gave interviewers a straight answer; once he described himself as "just a song and dance man."

207

rather than belief; by what they don't know [rather] than by what they do."

To give Bob Dylan his due, one must remember that throughout his career, he has always been a true spiritual seeker and he has always revealed an insistent and powerful moral, religious, and even apocalyptic and messianic consciousness (think of songs such as "I'd Hate to Be You on That Dreadful Day," "Masters of War," "A Hard Rain's A-Gonna Fall," "When the Ship Comes In," "Highway 61 Revisited," "Father of the Night," "I Shall Be Released," "Quinn the Eskimo," "Shelter from the Storm" and "Oh, Sister"). Exile, redemption, salvation, righteousness, judgment, faith and belief had all been constant concerns and themes in his work. And he has always sung of Jesus—the greatest of Dylan's outlaw heroes—as one of the principled teachers and healers of the world who was unjustly scorned, abused and misunderstood.

And again, to give the angel his due, one must say that *Slow Train Coming* is probably the best produced and most polished album Dylan ever made, is musically on a very high level, and communicates sparks of authentic spiritual feeling and passion in songs like "Precious Angel," "I Believe in You," and the *sui generis* "Man Gave Names to All the Animals"—his most delightful children's song since "Forever Young." But *Saved* and *Shot of Love* (with the radiant exception of the latter's "Every Grain of Sand") too often convey a sense of bathos, self-justification and ill-temper. Even as moving a song as "Covenant Woman" (on *Saved*) is sung in a tone that suggests enervation rather than exaltation. Rarely on these last two albums do you find the joyfulness of a great gospel singer like Marion Williams or the clarity and charity of a recording I've heard of an elderly Shaker woman singing by herself, in a very tiny voice, a version of the beautiful hymn " 'Tis the Gift to Be Simple." And when Dylan portentously an-

Preceding page: The Rolling Thunder Revue gave a benefit at Madison Square Garden for Rubin "Hurricane" Carter, a former boxer (right), allegedly framed on a murder charge. Left: With Patti Smith. This page and following: With the Band in scenes from The Last Waltz, *Martin Scorsese's documentary of the Band's farewell concert in San Francisco.*

211

Dylan was spotted by a
policeman outside the Roxy
theater in Los Angeles, where
Ronee Blakley was
performing in March 1977.

214

"to protect
and to serve"

nounced, as he did during one of his 1979 concerts in San Francisco, that "this concert is brought to you under the authorization of Jesus Christ," I think it is fair to say that he had become a radically different kind of person from the one we used to know. It was almost as if he had once again decided to change his name.

But not quite. Ultimately true to himself, Bob Dylan has always remained a creature of change ("Change: that is the unchangeable"); as he once told an interviewer: "There comes a time for all things to pass." Like the god Proteus, Dylan had been held still for about three years and had become a born-again prophet. But whenever Dylan had previously felt confined, trapped, stalled or locked in some aesthetic or ideological vault, he had always rebelled ("An' I'll sing my song like a rebel wild / For it's that I am an' can't deny," he had written in his liner notes for *Joan Baez in Concert, Part 2*).

One might have seen a sign of his incipient rebellion in the extraordinary, visionary, still-unreleased song "Caribbean Wind" (with its images of "the furnace of desire" and "ships of liberty"), which Dylan had sung only at certain of his concerts between 1980 and 1981—a song that broke with the generally rigid versifying and moralizing of his born-again compositions and returned to the leaping verbal associations and passionate allusiveness of earlier songwriting periods. But it was the release of his album *Infidels* in late 1983 that revealed the unmistakable loosening of the born-again, Protean grip. As he sang on "Don't Fall Apart on Me Tonight": "It's like I'm stuck inside a painting / That's hanging in the Louvre / My throat starts to tickle and my nose itches / But I know that I can't move." And as he allegorically criticized the archetypal fundamentalist ideologue in "Man of Peace": "He's a great humanitarian, he's a great philanthropist / He knows just where to touch you, honey, and how you like to be kissed / He'll put both his

In 1977 Dylan's wife, Sara, divorced him after twelve years of marriage. The personal trauma was followed by artistic failure: his four-hour movie, Renaldo and Clara, *was savaged by critics and ignored by an uncomprehending public.*

216

arms around you / You can feel the tender touch of the beast / You know that sometimes Satan comes as a man of peace." It was in this same song that Dylan hinted that it was in a time of personal hopelessness and weakness that he had earlier gotten ideologically caught ("Well, he catch you when you're hoping for a glimpse of the sun / Catch you when your troubles feel like they weigh a ton"). But it is important to point out that *Infidels* hardly indicated a new "atheistic" Dylan. On the contrary, the album suggested a swerving away from an adherence to a limited and limiting "creed" ("Today's religion is tomorrow's bondage," he told *City Pages* at the time of the album's release) but, at the same time, emphasized a commitment (always present in Dylan's work) to a *truly* religious sense of life—one shorn of platitudes and illusions. And Dylan communicated this in a record that was musically intense and alive. As he had once written in *11 Outlined Epitaphs:*

there's a movie called
Shoot the Piano Player
the last line proclaimin'
"music, man, that's where it's at"
it is a religious line
outside, the chimes rung
an' they
    are still ringin'

And the chimes can certainly be heard ringing from the first bars of the album's first song, "Jokerman." Accompanied by a brilliant band led by guitarist Mark Knopfler, Dylan radiates a musical energy and vocal expression that often reminds one of *Highway 61 Revisited, Blonde on Blonde, The Basement Tapes* and *Blood on the Tracks.* But like the symbolic Jester or Clown or Joker who tells terrible things lightly, *Infidel's* musical exuberance cannot disguise its ultimately dark concern—the tragic infidelities, on all levels, of contemporary life. In fact, the songs on the album remind us of the no-exit loft of "Visions of

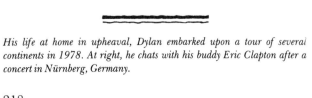

His life at home in upheaval, Dylan embarked upon a tour of several continents in 1978. At right, he chats with his buddy Eric Clapton after a concert in Nürnberg, Germany.

218

In the first half of 1978 Bob Dylan performed to sell-out crowds in Japan, Australia, and across Europe. Preceding page and at right: On the European leg of the tour.

Chastened by the disappointing reception of Renaldo and Clara, *and then* Street-Legal, *on his 1978 tour Dylan was trying to please his audience, joking and talking to them between songs.*

Johanna," where, as Dylan once sang, "we sit here stranded, though we're all doin' our best to deny it." But the "loft" has not become the "world"—one filled with pagan, idol-worshiping saviors ("Jokerman"), false ideologues ("Man of Peace"), beautiful spirits in a spiritual wasteland ("Sweetheart Like You"), men and women unable to communicate with each other ("I and I," "Don't Fall Apart on Me Tonight"), and human beings caught in a trap of their own making ("License to Kill"). This last song is one of Dylan's greatest works—nothing less than a view of the state of modern man who, "afraid and confused," is "set on a path where he's bound to get ill," and who, "hell bent for destruction," worships his reflection "at an altar of a stagnant pool." Years ago, Dylan had given us a similar picture of deluded man in songs like "Subterranean Homesick Blues" and "It's Alright, Ma." But there is no Chuck Berry–like gaiety or rebellious breathlessness in "License to Kill." In its slow, haunted poetry and musical transparency it resembles much more the unreleased Basement Tapes version of "Too Much of Nothing" ("Too much of nothing / Can turn a man into a liar, / It can cause one man to sleep on nails / And another man to eat fire"); but it supersedes that song in the way it sees man's irreparable lack of humility, false values, ignorance, narcissism and selfishness as leading to the possibility of self-inflicted, worldwide extermination. And at the moral center of this amazing song is the "woman on my block"—an imperturbable, primordial figure like one of the Fates who, as "the night grows still," is a witness to our personal, political and spiritual insanity.

(It should be mentioned that in the two most polemical and specifically ideological songs on *Infidels*—"Neighborhood Bully" and "Union Sundown"—Dylan's musical passion and poetic irony make him overlook other equally important ironies. The former song—a barely disguised defense of the state of Israel—contains lines like: "He's wandered the earth an exiled man / Seen his family scattered, his people hounded and torn" that could be applied not only to the Jewish people throughout history but also to today's Palestinians; and the latter song—a diatribe against greed, in this case of the American labor unions—neglects to take into account the recent loss of many union jobs, forced cuts in union pay, the continuing exploitation of migrant workers and the reemergence of sweatshops in our larger cities.)

But *Infidels*, in any case, is truly a collection of Dylan's Songs of Experience. And as William Blake asked: "What is the price of Experience? Do men buy it for a song? / Or wisdom for a dance in the street? No, it is bought with the price / Of all that a man hath, his house, his wife, his children. / Wisdom is sold in the desolate market where none come to buy, / And in the wither'd field where the farmer plows for bread in vain." For on *Infidels*, Dylan has returned, vulnerable and raw, to our world of chaos, "still pushin' myself along the road" and walking "barefoot," as he tells us in "I and I."

In his born-again song "Precious Angel" (from *Slow Train*), Dylan sang: "Ya either got faith or ya got unbelief and there ain't no neutral ground." These were, of course, the positions represented by the Thief and the Joker in "All Along the Watchtower." But throughout Dylan's career, there has been a tension between the imperatives of enlightenment and salvation, of consciousness and conscience; between the reality of life's confusions and his personal need for certainty; between his unflinching observation of the chaos of the world and his sometimes desperate search for something to live up to and believe in; between being a "dream twister" ("Jokerman") and a truth-seeker.

On the album cover of *Infidels*, we see Bob Dylan's face in black glasses, impermeable, inscrutable and in the masked darkness of a personal exile. (Again, we are reminded that the man in the mask is able both to hide and to

Dylan's 1978 tour disappointed many of his longtime fans and infuriated rock critics. His older songs had been drastically rearranged, and his band, complete with a saxophonist, a conga drummer, and a trio of back-up singers, left many listeners feeling bewildered. The rebel of the Sixties seemed to be retreating from his former iconoclastic stance, and his concerts were derided by some observers as the "Las Vegas" tour.

Dylan, as usual, ignored his critics. He performed the new "big band" arrangements of his most popular songs in sold-out arenas throughout the country, 1978.

*Dylan onstage in Blackbush,
England, 1978, his last
European appearance.*

The back cover of Shot of Love, *the third Bob Dylan album of Christian songs, portrayed him seemingly at peace with himself, admiring a rose.*

234

*Dylan's house in Malibu,
under construction in 1976.
Following pages: Dylan
appeared at the bar mitzvah of
one of his sons in Jerusalem in
1983.*

236

unmask those around him.) But on the inside record sleeve there is a beautiful photograph of a shadeless Bob Dylan—looking graceful and at one with the world—crouching on the slope of a rocky, dusty hill overlooking the city of Jerusalem at dawn. He is examining a stone of the "Holy City of Peace," which is an *idea* (*Jerusalem* was, for example, William Blake's word for *liberty*) as well as a *place*—a celestial as well as an earthly city dreamed about and fought over for centuries by diverse peoples and religions.

At the time of this writing, it was being reported that Dylan had been spending time in Jerusalem and was deeply involved with the Lubavitch movement, the traditionalist, ultra-orthodox Hasidic Jewish sect based in Brooklyn, New York. Robert Zimmerman had been, of course, brought up as a Jew in Hibbing and had had his bar mitzvah there in 1954. In addition, according to Stephen Pickering—who has written several books on the singer as a "Jewish Poet in Search of God"—Bob Dylan, in the early Seventies, studied with a rabbi in New York, visited Israel several times, thought of settling there and even applied for membership on a kibbutz. But according to Toby Thompson, Mrs. Beatty Zimmerman informed him that "as a child, Bob attended *all* the churches around Hibbing; he was very interested in religion, and *all* religions, by no means just his own." And as Dylan himself told *Playboy* in 1978: "I don't really consider myself Jewish or non-Jewish. . . . I'm not a patriot to any creed. I believe in all of them and none of them. A devout Christian or Moslem can be just as effective as a devout Jew."

Now, in 1983, Dylan was reemphasizing his elemental—if not institutional—identification as a Jew in a remarkable confession in *City Pages*: "My so-called Jewish roots are in Egypt. They went down there with Joseph, and they came back out with Moses, you know, the guy that killed the Egyptian, married an Ethiopian girl and brought the law down from the mountain. The same Moses whose staff turned into a serpent. The same person who killed three thousand Hebrews for getting down, stripping off their clothes and dancing around a golden calf. . . . Roots, man—we're talking about Jewish roots, you want to know more? Check up on Elijah the prophet. He could make rain. Isaiah the prophet, even Jeremiah—see if their brethren didn't want to bust their brains for telling it right like it is, yeah—these are my roots, I suppose. Am I looking for them? Well, I don't know. I ain't looking for them in synagogues with six pointed Egyptian stars shining down from every window, I can tell you that much."

In thinking about Bob Dylan and his protean and mercurial ways, I'm reminded of a saying of the late-eighteenth-century Hasidic master Rabbi Nachman of Bratzlav: "The world is like a revolving die, and everything turns over, and man changes to angel and angel to man, and the head to the foot and the foot to the head. So all things turn over and revolve and are changed, this into that and that into this, what is above to what is beneath and what is beneath to what is above. For in the root all is one, and in the transformation and return of things redemption is enclosed."

And in thinking of Bob Dylan and his concern with the conflict between faith and unbelief, I'm reminded of a poem by the eleventh-century Perisan Sufi poet and philosopher Omar Khayyam (as translated by Peter Avery and John Heath-Stubbs):

My rule of life is to drink and be merry,
To be free from belief and unbelief is my religion:
I asked the Bride of Destiny her bride-price,
"Your joyous heart," she said.

"I gave her my heart but she wanted my soul," Bob Dylan sang in one of his most famous early songs ("Don't Think Twice, It's All Right"); and as he sang in one of his most recent ones, "Someone else is speakin' with my mouth, but I'm listening only to my heart" ("I and I").

And as Bob Dylan continues onward in his earthly and spiritual journey, we should remember, as we allow the soul to find its way, to be thankful for all of the joyous songs from the heart that this extraordinary artist has given us ever since he busily began being born and born again.

Lad of Athens, faithful be
To Thyself,
And Mystery—
All the rest is Perjury—

—Emily Dickinson

DISCOGRAPHY

BOB DYLAN
March 1962 (Columbia)

You're No Good (Jesse Fuller); Talkin' New York; In My Time of Dyin' (Jesus Gonna Make Up My Dyin' Bed) (Blind Willie Johnson); Man of Constant Sorrow (trad., arr. Bob Dylan); Fixin' to Die (Bukka White); Pretty Peggy-O (trad., arr. Bob Dylan); Highway 51 (Curtis Jones); Gospel Plow (trad., arr. Bob Dylan); Baby, Let Me Follow You Down (Eric von Schmidt); House of the Risin' Sun (trad.); Freight Train Blues (Roy Acuff); Song to Woody; See That My Grave Is Kept Clean (Blind Lemon Jefferson)

THE FREEWHEELIN' BOB DYLAN
May 1963 (Columbia)

Blowin' in the Wind; Girl from the North Country; Masters of War; Down the Highway; Bob Dylan's Blues; A Hard Rain's A-Gonna Fall; Don't Think Twice, It's All Right; Bob Dylan's Dream; Oxford Town; Talkin' World War III Blues; Corrina, Corrina (trad., arr. Bob Dylan); Honey, Just Allow Me One More Chance (Henry Thomas/Bob Dylan); I Shall Be Free

THE TIMES THEY ARE A-CHANGIN'
January 1964 (Columbia)

The Times They Are A-Changin'; Ballad of Hollis Brown; With God on Our Side; One Too Many Mornings; North Country Blues; Only a Pawn in Their Game; Boots of Spanish Leather; When the Ship Comes In; The Lonesome Death of Hattie Carroll; Restless Farewell

ANOTHER SIDE OF BOB DYLAN
August 1964 (Columbia)

All I Really Want to Do; Black Crow Blues; Spanish Harlem Incident; Chimes of Freedom; I Shall Be Free No. 10; To Ramona; Motorpsycho Nitemare; My Back Pages; I Don't Believe You; Ballad in Plain D; It Ain't Me Babe

BRINGING IT ALL BACK HOME
March 1965 (Columbia)

Subterranean Homesick Blues; She Belongs to Me; Maggie's Farm; Love Minus Zero/No Limit; Outlaw Blues;

Excluding bootlegs.

On the Road Again; Bob Dylan's 115th Dream; Mr. Tambourine Man; Gates of Eden; It's Alright, Ma (I'm Only Bleeding); It's All Over Now, Baby Blue

HIGHWAY 61 REVISITED
August 1965 (Columbia)

Like a Rolling Stone; Tombstone Blues; It Takes a Lot to Laugh, It Takes a Train to Cry; From a Buick 6; Ballad of a Thin Man; Queen Jane Approximately; Highway 61 Revisited; Just Like Tom Thumb's Blues; Desolation Row

BLONDE ON BLONDE
May 1966 (Columbia)

Rainy Day Women #12 & 35; Pledging My Time; Visions of Johanna; One of Us Must Know (Sooner or Later); I Want You; Stuck Inside of Mobile with the Memphis Blues Again; Leopardskin Pill-Box Hat; Just Like a Woman; Most Likely You Go Your Way and I'll Go Mine; Temporary Like Achilles; Absolutely Sweet Marie; 4th Time Around; Obviously 5 Believers; Sad-Eyed Lady of the Lowlands

BOB DYLAN'S GREATEST HITS
March 1967 (Columbia)

Rainy Day Women #12 & 35; Blowin' in the Wind; The Times They Are A-Changin'; It Ain't Me Babe; Like a Rolling Stone; Mr. Tambourine Man; Subterranean Homesick Blues; Positively 4th Street; I Want You; Just Like a Woman

JOHN WESLEY HARDING
December 1967 (Columbia)

John Wesley Harding; As I Went Out One Morning; I Dreamed I Saw St. Augustine; All Along the Watchtower; The Ballad of Frankie Lee and Judas Priest; Drifter's Escape; Dear Landlord; I Am a Lonesome Hobo; I Pity the Poor Immigrant; The Wicked Messenger; Down Along the Cove; I'll Be Your Baby Tonight

NASHVILLE SKYLINE
April 1969 (Columbia)

Girl from the North Country; Nashville Skyline Rag (instrumental); To

Be Alone With You; I Threw It All Away; Peggy Day; Lay Lady Lay; One More Night; Tell Me That It Isn't True; Country Pie; Tonight I'll Be Staying Here With You

SELF PORTRAIT
June 1970 (Columbia)

All the Tired Horses; Alberta #1 (Leadbelly, registered as Bob Dylan); I Forgot More Than You'll Ever Know (Cecil A. Null); Days of 49 (I. Warner/ J. A. Lomax/A. Lomax); Early Mornin' Rain (Gordon Lightfoot); In Search of Little Sadie (trad., registered as Bob Dylan); Let It Be Me (Pierre Delanoé/ Gilbert Bécaud/M. Curtis); Little Sadie (trad., registered as Bob Dylan); Woogie-Boogie (instrumental); Belle Isle (trad., registered as Bob Dylan); Living the Blues; Like a Rolling Stone; Copper Kettle (The Pale Moonlight) (trad.); Gotta Travel On (Paul Clayton/Larry Ehrlich/David Lazar/Tom Six); Blue Moon (Lorenz Hart/Richard Rodgers); The Boxer (Paul Simon); The Mighty Quinn (Quinn, the Eskimo); Take Me As I Am (Or Let Me Go) (Boudleaux Bryant); Take a Message to Mary (Felice and Boudleaux Bryant); It Hurts Me Too (Tampa Red); Minstrel Boy; She Belongs to Me; Wigwam (instrumental); Alberta #2 (Leadbelly, registered as Bob Dylan)

NEW MORNING
October 1970 (Columbia)

If Not for You; Day of the Locusts; Time Passes Slowly; Went to See the Gypsy; Winterlude; If Dogs Run Free; New Morning; Sign on the Window; One More Weekend; The Man in Me; Three Angels; Father of Night

BOB DYLAN'S GREATEST HITS, VOLUME II
November 1971 (Columbia)

Watching the River Flow; Don't Think Twice, It's All Right; Lay Lady Lay; Stuck Inside of Mobile with the Memphis Blues Again; I'll Be Your Baby Tonight; All I Really Want to Do; My Back Pages; Maggie's Farm; Tonight I'll Be Staying Here with You; She Belongs to Me; All Along the Watchtower; The Mighty Quinn (Quinn, the Eskimo); Just Like Tom Thumb's Blues; A Hard Rain's A-Gonna Fall; If

Not for You; It's All Over Now, Baby Blue; Tomorrow's a Long Time; When I Paint My Masterpiece; I Shall Be Released; You Ain't Goin' Nowhere; Down in the Flood

PAT GARRETT & BILLY THE KID

July 1973 (Columbia)

Main Theme (Billy) (instrumental); Cantina Theme (Working for the Law) (instrumental); Billy 1; Bunkhouse Theme (instrumental); River Theme; Turkey Chase (instrumental); Knockin' on Heaven's Door; Final Theme; Billy 4; Billy 7

DYLAN

November 1973 (Columbia)

Lily of the West (Flora) (E. Davis/J. Peterson); Can't Help Falling in Love (George Weiss/Hugo Peretti/Luigi Creatore); Sarah Jane (trad.); The Ballad of Ira Hayes (Peter La Farge); Mr. Bojangles (Jerry Jeff Walker); Mary Ann (trad.); Big Yellow Taxi (Joni Mitchell); A Fool Such As I (Bill Trader); Spanish Is the Loving Tongue (Charles Badger Clark)

PLANET WAVES

January 1974 (Asylum)

On a Night like This; Going Going Gone; Tough Mama; Hazel; Something There Is About You; Forever Young; Forever Young; Dirge; You Angel You; Never Say Goodbye; Wedding Song

BEFORE THE FLOOD

June 1974 (Asylum)

Most Likely You Go Your Way and I'll Go Mine; Lay Lady Lay; Rainy Day Women #12 & 35; Knockin' on Heaven's Door; It Ain't Me Babe; Ballad of a Thin Man; Don't Think Twice, It's All Right; Just Like a Woman; It's Alright, Ma (I'm Only Bleeding); All Along the Watchtower; Highway 61 Revisited; Like a Rolling Stone; Blowin' in the Wind

BLOOD ON THE TRACKS

January 1975 (Columbia)

Tangled Up in Blue; Simple Twist of Fate; You're a Big Girl Now; Idiot Wind; You're Gonna Make Me Lonesome When You Go; Meet Me in the Morning; Lily, Rosemary and the Jack of Hearts; If You See Her, Say Hello; Shelter from the Storm; Buckets of Rain

THE BASEMENT TAPES

June 1975 (Columbia)

Odds and Ends; Orange Juice Blues (Blues for Breakfast) (Richard Manuel); Million Dollar Bash; Yazoo

Street Scandal (Robbie Robertson); Goin' to Acapulco; Katie's Been Gone (Robbie Robertson/Richard Manuel); Lo and Behold!; Bessie Smith (Rick Danko/Robbie Robertson); Clothes Line Saga; Apple Suckling Tree; Please, Mrs. Henry; Tears of Rage (Bob Dylan/Richard Manuel); Too Much of Nothing; Yea! Heavy and a Bottle of Bread; Ain't No More Cane (trad., arr. by The Band); Crash on the Levee (Down in the Flood); Ruben Remus (Robbie Robertson/Richard Manuel); Tiny Montgomery; You Ain't Goin' Nowhere; Don't Ya Tell Henry; Nothing Was Delivered; Open the Door, Homer; Long Distance Operator; This Wheel's on Fire (Bob Dylan/Rick Danko)

DESIRE

January 1976 (Columbia)

Hurricane (Bob Dylan/Jacques Levy); Isis (Bob Dylan/Jacques Levy); Mozambique (Bob Dylan/Jacques Levy); One More Cup of Coffee; Oh, Sister (Bob Dylan/Jacques Levy); Joey (Bob Dylan/Jacques Levy); Romance in Durango (Bob Dylan/Jacques Levy); Black Diamond Bay (Bob Dylan/Jacques Levy); Sara

HARD RAIN

September 1976 (Columbia)

Maggie's Farm; One Too Many Mornings; Stuck Inside of Mobile with the Memphis Blues Again; Oh, Sister (Bob Dylan/Jacques Levy); Lay Lady Lay; Shelter from the Storm; You're a Big Girl Now; I Threw It All Away; Idiot Wind

MASTERPIECES

March 1978 (CBS/Sony, released in Japan)

Knockin' on Heaven's Door; Mr. Tambourine Man; Just Like a Woman; I Shall Be Released; Tears of Rage; All Along the Watchtower; One More Cup of Coffee; Like a Rolling Stone; The Mighty Quinn (Quinn the Eskimo); Tomorrow's a Long Time; Lay Lady Lay; Idiot Wind; Mixed Up Confusion; Positively 4th Street; Can You Please Crawl Out Your Window; Just Like Tom Thumb's Blues; Spanish Is the Loving Tongue (Charles Badger Clark); George Jackson (big band version); Rita Mae (Bob Dylan/Jacques Levy); Blowin' in the Wind; A Hard Rain's A-Gonna Fall; The Times They Are A-Changin'; Masters of War; Hurricane (Bob Dylan/Jacques Levy); Maggie's Farm; Subterranean Homesick Blues; Ballad of a Thin Man; Mozambique (Bob Dylan/Jacques Levy); This Wheel's On Fire (Bob Dylan/Rick Danko); I Want You; Rainy Day Women #12 & 35; Don't Think Twice, It's All Right; Song to Woody;

It Ain't Me Babe; Love Minus Zero/No Limit; I'll Be Your Baby Tonight; If Not For You; If You See Her, Say Hello; Sara

BOB DYLAN AT BUDOKAN

May 1978 (Columbia)

Mr. Tambourine Man; Shelter from the Storm; Love Minus Zero/No Limit; Ballad of a Thin Man; Don't Think Twice, It's All Right; Maggie's Farm; One More Cup of Coffee; Like a Rolling Stone; I Shall Be Released; Is Your Love in Vain?; Going Going Gone; Blowin' in the Wind; Just Like a Woman; Oh, Sister (Bob Dylan/Jacques Levy); Simple Twist of Fate; All Along the Watchtower; I Want You; All I Really Want to Do; Knockin' on Heaven's Door; It's Alright, Ma (I'm Only Bleeding); Forever Young; The Times They Are A-Changin'

STREET LEGAL

June 1978 (Columbia)

Changing of the Guards; New Pony; No Time to Think; Baby Stop Crying; Is Your Love in Vain?; Señor (Tales of Yankee Power); True Love Tends to Forget; We Better Talk This Over; Where Are You Tonight? (Journey through Dark Heat)

SLOW TRAIN COMING

August 1979 (Columbia)

Gotta Serve Somebody; Precious Angel; I Believe in You; Slow Train; Gonna Change My Way of Thinking; Do Right to Me Baby (Do Unto Others); When You Gonna Wake Up; Man Gave Names to All the Animals; When He Returns

SAVED

June 1980 (Columbia)

A Satisfied Mind (Red Hayes/Jack Rhodes); Saved (Bob Dylan/Tim Drummond); Covenant Woman; What Can I Do For You?; Solid Rock; Pressing On; In the Garden; Saving Grace; Are You Ready

SHOT OF LOVE

July 1981 (Columbia)

Shot of Love; Heart of Mine; Property of Jesus; Lenny Bruce; Watered-Down Love; Dead Man, Dead Man; In the Summertime; Trouble; Every Grain of Sand

INFIDELS

October 1983 (Columbia)

Jokerman; Sweetheart Like You; Neighborhood Bully; License to Kill; Man of Peace; Union Sundown; I and I; Don't Fall Apart on Me Tonight

CREDITS

(Page x) Neal Peters Collection; (2–3) *Minneapolis Star & Tribune*; (4) John Cohen; (5) John Cohen, courtesy of *Sing Out!* magazine; (6–7) *Minneapolis Star & Tribune*; (8) Woody Guthrie Publications, Inc.; (9) Jim Marshall; (10–11) Sam Falk/Monkmeyer Press Photo; (12) Jim Cron/Monkmeyer Press Photo; (13) David Gahr; (14–15) Gin Briggs/Fred W. McDarrah; (16, 17) David Gahr; (18–19) Joe Alper, courtesy of *Sing Out!* magazine and Jackie Gibson Alper; (20) CBS, Inc.; (21) Michael Ochs Archive; (22) Joe Alper, courtesy of Jackie Gibson Alper; (23, 24, 25) Michael Ochs Archive; (26–27) ©Daniel Kramer 1978; (28–29) John Launois/Black Star;(30–31, 32) Jim Marshall; (34) Frank Driggs Collection; (35) ©Daniel Kramer 1978; (36–37, 38) John Cohen; (39) AP/Wide World Photo; (40) courtesy of Michael Gross; (41) Joe Alper, courtesy of *Sing Out!* magazine; (42–43) Fred W. McDarrah; (44–45, 46, 47) Jim Marshall; (48–49) David Gahr; (50–51, 52, 53, 54–55) Jim Marshall; (56–57, 58–59, 60 left, 60–61, 63, 64–65) David Gahr; (68) Fred W. McDarrah; (69) Charles Harbutt/Archive; (70–71) Jim Marshall; (72, 73, 74–75) Danny Lyon/Magnum; (76, 77) ©Daniel Kramer 1965; (78, 79, 80–81) Fred W. McDarrah; (82–83) ©Daniel Kramer 1978; (84) ©Daniel Kramer 1966; (86, 87) Frank Driggs Collection; (88–89, 90–91) ©Daniel Kramer 1978; (92–93, 94–95) ©Daniel Kramer 1967; (96, 97) John Launois/Black Star; (98–99) ©Daniel Kramer 1967; (100–101) ©Daniel Kramer 1978; (102–103, 104–105, 106–107, 108–109) David Gahr; (110–111) ©Daniel Kramer 1978; (112–113) ©Daniel Kramer 1967; (114–115) Jim Marshall; (116–117) Larry Keenan, Jr.; (118–119, 120, 121) Nat Finkelstein; (123) Photo Trends; (124) Pennebaker Associates, Inc.; (125) courtesy of Michael Gross; (126) RDR Productions; (127, 129) courtesy of Michael Gross; (130) United Press International; (131) Photo Reporters; (132–133) United Press International; (134–135) Monique Valentin/Photo Reporters; (136–137) Pictorial Parade; (138–139) Nik Cohn and Guy Peelaert; (140–141) Monique Valentin/Photo Reporters, courtesy of Michael Gross; (143) courtesy of *Sing Out!* magazine; (144–145, 146–147) Elliott Landy; (148–149) Daniel Chidester, Image Works; (150–151, 152–153, 154–155, 156–157) Elliott Landy; (158–159) courtesy of Michael Gross; (160–161) David Gahr; (162–163) Jim Marshall; (164) RDR Productions; (165) Keystone Press Agency; (166–167) Photo Trends; (169) AP/Wide World Photo; (170–171) United Press International; (174–175) Bob Gruen/Starfile; (176–177) John Cohen; (178–179) United Press International; (180–181) Elliott Landy/Magnum; (182–183) Tom Zimberoff/Contact; (184, 185, 186–187) Michael Zagaris; (188–189) Bob Gruen/Starfile; (190) Elsa Dorfman; (191) Joseph Sia; (192–193, 194–195, 196–197) Ken Regan/Camera 5; (198–199) Elsa Dorfman; (200–201) Ken Regan/Camera 5; (202–203) Joseph Sia; (204–205) Retna Ltd.; (206, 207) Annie Leibovitz; (208) Ken Regan/Camera 5; (209) Charlyn Zlotnik; (210–211, 212–213) Neal Preston; (214–215) Ron Galella; (216–217) Annie Leibovitz; (218–219, 220–221, 222–223) Morgan Renaud/Sygma; (224–225) Waring Abbot; (226–227) Morgan Renaud/Sygma; (229) Waring Abbot; (230) David Gahr; (231) Stephen J. Shermer; (232–233) Sipa Press/Black Star; (234–235) Howard Alk; (236–237, 238–239) AP/Wide World Photos; (245) Ron Galella; (246) Ken Regan/Camera 5; (end papers) Howard Alk. Hand tinting on 6–7, 86–87, 200–201, and 220–221 by Leslie Fratkin.

PHOTO EDITOR ILENE CHERNA

This book was typeset by The Seven Graphic Arts, Inc. of New York, and printed by the web offset process by W.A. Krueger of New Berlin, Wisc.